THE INTELLIGENT INVESTOR

A Summary of
Benjamin Graham's original work

100 PAGE SUMMARIES

By Preston Pysh and Stig Brodersen

The Intelligent Investor 100 page summaries
copyright © by 100 page summaries.

All rights reserved.
Printed in the United States of America.

ISBN: 978-1-939370-11-2

Library of Congress Cataloging-in-Publication Data

Pysh, Preston and Brodersen, Stig
The Intelligent Investor
A Summary of Benjamin Graham's original work

This publication is designed to provide accurate and authoritative information
in regard to the subject matter covered. It is sold with the understanding that
neither the author nor the publisher is a registered expert in the subject
matter discussed. If legal advice or other expert assistance is required, the
services of a competent professional person should be sought.

Table of Contents

PREFACE TO THE FOURTH EDITION
– by WARREN E. BUFFETT

In the preface to the book, Warren Buffett talks about his experience with reading this book. His points are very straightforward:

- Investing doesn't require a super-high IQ.
- Successful investing is the result of implementing a sound strategy and being able to control your emotions. This book provides the strategy; you need to provide the emotional control.
- Pay special attention to chapters 8 and 20.
- Outstanding results depend on three factors: effort, intellect/ research, and the number of market swings you get the opportunity to experience. With respect to the last point, Graham's book will help you profit from market swings as opposed to participate in them.

INTRODUCTION
What This Book Expects to Accomplish

This is not a *"How to Make a Million Dollars"* kind of book.

The objectives of the book are:

1. To advise the reader against areas in which substantial error could occur.
2. To develop policies that are comfortable.
3. To supply guidance in the adoption and execution of an investment policy.
4. To supply guidance in a form suitable to the layperson.
5. To direct attention to the principles of investment and to the attitudes of investors.

Little will be said about the technique of analyzing securities, but, through the use of examples, the elements involved in making a wise choice will be brought home. Heeding the warning, "Those who do not remember the past are condemned to repeating it," attention is given in the book to historical patterns of financial markets. The book uses past decades to explain how the various types of bonds and stocks have behaved under varying conditions, some of which are likely to occur again.

The book has been written with investors in mind, as opposed to speculators, and the first task is to distinguish between the two. The underlying principles of sound investment should not alter from decade to decade, but the application of these principles must be adapted to significant changes in the financial mechanisms and climate. Always remember; enthusiasm on Wall Street almost invariably leads to disaster!

The book distinguishes between two types of investor:

- The defensive or passive investor, who primarily emphasizes the avoidance of losses; he does not wish to spend time making frequent decisions.
- The enterprising, active or aggressive investor, who is willing to devote the necessary time and care to the selection of sound

securities that are more attractive than the average; he might, over decades, expect a better return than that of the passive investor.

The art of successful investment is based on first selecting the industry that is most likely to grow, then selecting the most promising company within that industry—Graham cites computers and IBM as his examples. He also points, however, to his own 1949 recommendation that air-transport stocks had a "brilliant" future, although, as it turned out, the industry grew but many of the individual stocks did very badly. Graham consents that although IBM has done very well, many other companies in that industry have not. (In 2012, *Fortune* ranked IBM the second-largest U.S. firm in terms of number of employees, the fourth-largest in terms of market capitalization, and the ninth most profitable.)

The following lessons can be drawn from this:

1. Obvious indications for growth in a business do not necessarily turn into obvious profits for investors.
2. Just because they are "experts" does not mean they have dependable ways of selecting promising companies in promising industries.

The investor's chief problem, and his worst enemy, is likely to be himself, as he is exposed to the excitement and temptations of the stock market. Through this book, Graham hoped to instill in the reader the proper mental and emotional attitudes to adopt when making investment decisions.

The intent is to teach the reader to measure and quantify. At some prices, 99% of issues are cheap enough to buy. But the habit of relating what is being paid to what is being offered is an invaluable trait in investment: buy stocks as if they were groceries, not perfume! The really dreadful losses arose because the buyer forgot to ask, "How much is it worth?"

A creditable but unspectacular result can be achieved by the lay investor with minimum effort and capability. Bringing in knowledge and cleverness, however, is likely to worsen the situation.

Throughout the book, emphasis is placed on the virtues of having a simple portfolio: high-grade bonds and diversified leading common stocks. Beyond that, the path is challenging and difficult and the investor must be sure of himself and those who advise him. Investment must be based on the "margin of safety" principle.

The author's experience of the market began in 1914, before the start of the First World War. During the ensuing fifty-seven years, he experienced the ups and downs of the market—but he always remained confident that sound investment principles generally produced sound results.

CHAPTER 1
INVESTMENT VERSUS SPECULATION
RESULTS TO BE EXPECTED BY THE INTELLIGENT
INVESTOR

CHAPTER SUMMARY

In this chapter, Benjamin Graham distinguishes between speculators and investors. He makes it clear that the latter label is not suitable for everyone in the stock market. If an investor wants to participate in speculation, funds should be kept separate from those used for investing. Further, Benjamin Graham introduces the expectations for 'the defensive investor' who is investing in high-grade bonds and stable common stock. This type of portfolio could be managed by a third party. Contrarily, the 'aggressive investor' likes to work in active financial markets, expecting higher returns than those of his defensive counterparty. His methods include both trading and short selling of stocks.

CHAPTER OUTLINE

Investment Versus Speculation

In 1934, Graham tried to differentiate between investing and speculating by defining an investment as, "Promoting the safety of the principal and an adequate return," whereas a speculation fails to do either. But, because of historic collapses in the stock market, common stock—for some writers—became regarded as speculation. When the markets improved, the opposite occurred: all speculations became termed "investments," which gave rise to the oxymoron, "reckless investor."

The purpose of this book was to assist the reader to gain a clear idea of the risks inherent in ownership of common stocks, and to understand that the opportunities for profit are inseparable from risk: there is no such thing as a pure investment policy; there is always an element of speculation involved. The owner of the stocks must reduce risk and must be prepared financially and psychologically to face it.

Although the reader must accept that there is always an element of speculation, this can be reduced to "intelligent speculation" as opposed to the unintelligent speculator who believes that extreme levels are investments, and stakes more money than he can afford to lose. In this sense, buying "on margin" (a term for credit advanced by the broker to the purchaser, who is paying only a fraction of the full cost) is always speculation, and the broker has a legal requirement to advise his client of this fact. Although Graham recognizes, "Speculation is always fun," his advice to investors is to limit it to what you can afford to lose, to take out your winnings if you should have any, and to never confuse speculations and investments.

Results to be Expected by the Defensive Investor

The "defensive investor" combines the desire for safety with freedom from bother. What he can expect has changed over the years since Graham's book has been in circulation.

a) Recommendations in 1964

Divide holdings into at least 25% high-grade bonds and a minimum of 75% leading common stocks, preferably half of holdings in each. This was expected to give a 6% return, as well as the possibility of some capital appreciation.

b) Changes that had occurred by 1972

Interest rates on bonds had risen, and stock market values had fallen 38%. Graham recognizes that he—like everyone else—had not forecast the changes that occurred, and ruefully explained it as another of the endless experiences that show security prices are never predictable.

c) Expectations 1971-1972

The term "cash equivalents" is used for certain high-grade bonds guaranteed by government not to lose face value. The outlook for stocks versus bonds was less favorable than in 1964, leading to the suggestion that 100% of investment funds should be put into bonds, but with the warning that future inflation might make stocks preferable. Because of these and other potential changes, it was ultimately suggested that the fifty/fifty division between bonds and stocks was not unreasonable.

The likelihood of achieving better-than-average results by skillful investments is slight for both the individual and the professional manager of large funds. The contrary is likely to be true in pursuing quick profits; "Only rarely can one make dependable predictions about price changes."

The recommendations made are:

- Buy shares only from well established investment brokers
- If funds are substantial, employ a recognized investment counselor
- Employ *dollar cost averaging* with the same fixed amount of money in the same stock at fixed intervals.

Results to be Expected by the Aggressive Investor

The aggressive investor will expect to fare better than his passive equivalent, but his results may well be worse. By trading in the market, either in the short or long term, he will be competing with other investors who may be equally informed. The way to excel is to not follow the methods of the bulk of investors.

There was a time when the share value of a company was less than the value of the properties it owned, and in this case investments paid off; regretfully, such opportunities are now unusual. What remains for the aggressive investor is the search for undervalued and unrecognized companies with potential for improvement.

CHAPTER 2
THE INVESTOR AND INFLATION

CHAPTER SUMMARY

This chapter examines how inflation has diluted purchasing power, and what investors can do to prevent that. Inflationary impacts were compared between bonds and stocks; stocks proved to be the preferred choice though it has no certainty of adequate protection. Alternatives to common stock as an inflation protector were studied, including gold and real estate, but no alternatives were found to be better.

CHAPTER OUTLINE

The much-discussed inflation has resulted in the loss of the dollar, the loss of purchasing power, and the suffering of those on a fixed income. Stock value may possibly rise in step with inflation, which has led some advisers to conclude that bonds are less desirable since their face value will not be degraded.

Future policy must be based on past experience. Inflation is not new; the cost of living doubled between 1915 and 1920, but rose only 15% between 1965 and 1970. In the interim, there were three periods when prices declined and two when they rose. The average annual rate of inflation over twenty years (prior to publication in 1972) was 2.5%, and although Graham supposed governments would control inflation, the cost of living still doubled between 1973 and 1982.

This raises the question as to whether an investor could do better than high-grade bonds, given the inflation protection provided by many stocks. Between 1915 and 1970, the Dow Jones average of major companies' stocks rose by an annualized rate of 4%, and there was a further 4% value in company dividends, giving an annualized benefit of 8%. Although that rate was better than could have been obtained from bonds in the same period of time, it was not better than that offered by bonds at the time Graham was writing, in 1973.

Graham's answer to the question, "Are common stocks likely to do better in future than in the previous fifty-five years?" was a blunt no. There is no close connection in time between inflation/deflation and the price of common stocks.

Inflation and Corporate Earnings

The earnings rate of a company in proportion to its capital has not kept pace with inflation and the rising cost of living, and the investor should not expect a better return than 10% on book value (net asset value of a company's securities)—and more realistically, only 4%. In the past, inflation has not had any direct effect on a company's earnings, but the increased dollar value of shares on the Dow Jones is a result of reinvestment of earnings. Although business may appear to be better at times when there has been some slight inflation, this was not reflected in the earning power of capital, probably because the rise in wages exceeded the rise in productivity and because of the need for more capital investment. The net result has been a 500% expansion of debt due to inflation, and only a 200% increase in profit; there was no benefit to the shareholders from inflation.

Mounting debt has become a real problem: in 1950, corporate earnings before tax were 30% of debt; in 1969 this had fallen to 13.2%. Possibly earnings on equities are obtained at the expense of an increase in corporate debt.

The investor should not expect better than a return of 8% on his Dow Jones-listed stocks, but, based on the sage judgment of the market, "It will fluctuate," the investor should not expect uniform annual returns or growth; nor should he be led astray by out-of-the-ordinary advances and declines.

Alternatives to Common Stocks as Inflation Hedges

American citizens have been forbidden to hold gold metal since 1935. Although its value climbed from $35 to $48 per ounce in the thirty-five years prior to 1972, it gained no investment income and the holder of the gold would have done better with his money in a savings bank.

Although some persons have done very well from investments in art, jewelry, etc., this is not a market for the uninformed to venture into. Real estate, on the other hand, has been more reliable, though with its own fluctuations.

Conclusion

The investor should not put all his funds into one basket. The investor who depends on the income from his portfolio must guard against the unexpected and minimize his risk. <u>Although stocks are not an absolute protection against inflation, bonds can be expected to perform even worse than stocks.</u>

CHAPTER 3
A CENTURY OF STOCK MARKET HISTORY:
THE LEVEL OF STOCK PRICES IN EARLY 1972

CHAPTER SUMMARY

This chapter outlines the history of stock market performance, and Benjamin Graham stresses the importance of the investor being familiar with this. Caution is advised with regard to believing that markets will never turn down again—a popular opinion after long periods of above-average stock performance. Another aspect addressed here is the fact that, while timing of fluctuations in the stock market levels cannot be predicted, irrational behavior is often observed.

CHAPTER OUTLINE

An investor in the stock market should know something of its history, should know how stock values have advanced during the cycles of a century, and should learn the relationship between stock prices, earnings, and dividends.

In the century dated from 1871, there were nineteen bear (market declines) and bull (market advances) cycles. Three distinct periods emerged: in that of 1900-1924, there was a series of minor cycles of three to five years in duration and the market advanced an average of 3% per year; from 1924, there was initially a major bull market, followed by the collapse of historical proportions in 1929 then irregular fluctuations up until 1949, with an annualized rate of 1.5% gain; although there were major fluctuations until 1972, the annualized gain in value of stocks was 11%, dividends gave further value of 3.5%—a total of over 14% per year on average. All of which led some to believe it could never turn down—a very dangerous view to hold.

The Stock Market Level in 1972

The Dow Jones Industrial Average (DJIA) stood in 1948 at 180, and in 1972 at 900. In 1953, when it had advanced by 50% in five years, Graham advised caution, but the market defied his advice and went on to gain a further 100% in the next five years, until it stood at 584 in 1959. At this point Graham declared it "Dangerous." But the market kept climbing, reaching 685 in 1961. It then fell again, climbed again, then fell 27% in 1962, when IBM stocks fell by 50%, and those of less well-known companies fell by 90%. This was largely the result of the stocks having been pushed to illogical heights by speculators believing themselves to be investors. But the market recovered to 892 at the end of 1964, when Graham appeared confused by its behavior: "If the 1964 price level is not too high, how can we say *any* price level is too high?" And although it climbed to 839, in 1970 it was soon back to 632—lower than it had been throughout the six previous years.

In hindsight, Graham acknowledged his inability to "call the market," but believes his guiding principle of a constant investment policy that did not attempt to "beat the market" by "picking the winners" would have remained appropriate. He did, however, expect a further rise, "Far beyond the 900 DJIA level," and in January 2014 the DJIA stands at over 16,000.

CHAPTER 4
GENERAL PORTFOLIO POLICY:
THE DEFENSIVE INVESTOR

CHAPTER SUMMARY

This chapter explains why the allocation between stocks and bonds is easy to teach but hard to follow, due to human nature. The anticipated return is therefore a reflection of the defensive investor's intelligent effort. One indicator of changing capital allocation between DIJA and high- grade bonds is the earnings yield. Benjamin Graham discusses the subject of selecting bond investments, providing guidance based on the current (1972) investment opportunities for bonds.

CHAPTER OUTLINE

The characteristics of a portfolio reflect those of its owner. The principle to follow is: those who cannot afford risk should accept a low return. This does not mean the anticipated rate of return is directly related to risk. Instead, it should be related to the amount of intelligent effort behind the investment decision.

The Basic Problem of Bond-Stock Allocation

"Copybook maxims" suggest a basic fifty-fifty division between bonds and stocks. Instead, Graham suggests a holding between 25% and 75% depending on the market conditions; for example, at the bottom of a bear (depressed) market, an investor should increase their share of common stock so that it encompasses 75% of his portfolio, while bonds may make up only 25%. Such maxims are easy to teach and hard to follow since they go contrary to human nature, and it is human nature that drives the swings in the market. Indeed, the professional investors, with the mutual funds they direct, have not set an example.

This precaution has lost its followers; for example, directors of university endowment funds, some of whom have not been able to resist the temptations of the bull market. The truly conservative investor can at one side of the cycle enjoy the benefits of rising values, and at the other side of the cycle feel pleased about how little of his investment is declining in comparison with those of other, more aggressive, speculators.

A "buying point," when the investor switches from one component to the other, could be based on a comparison of Dow Jones expectations versus bond yields.

The Bond Component

This section provides guidance on a) taxable or tax-free bonds, and b) short- or long-term bonds (please remember this information is from the 1970s).

Whether to opt for taxable or tax-free bonds is an arithmetical problem that should be addressed to one's tax adviser, but the long versus short question should be addressed by the investor himself.

For the relatively small investor, US savings bonds are the ideal. For the larger wealth investor, some options are:

US Savings Bonds Series H: Pay interest semi-annually, 4.29% the first year, then 5.1% to maturity at ten years.

US Savings Bonds Series E: Sold at 75% face value; interest is not paid but accrues at 5% to maturity at five years and ten months, or rather less if redeemed earlier. There is no other investment that offers: absolute assurance of principle as well as interest payments; "money back" on demand; guaranteed 5% interest for at least ten years. Federal income tax is payable; State tax is not; tax is deferred in the Series E bonds.

Other United States Bonds: There are many varieties from which to choose; all are guaranteed by the Federal Government and subject to Federal but not State income tax, with the exception of housing authority bonds, which are tax exempt.

State and Municipal Bonds: Exempt from Federal income tax and usually exempt from State tax where issued, but not in other states. Their safety is variable, but the investor can be guided by the ratings agencies; an A rating is most likely safe.

Corporation Bonds: Subject to both Federal and State income tax.

Higher-Yielding Bond Investments: Higher yields correspond to lower safety ratings by the agencies, and the possibility of default is always to be balanced against the desirability of higher income.

Savings Deposits in Lieu of Bonds: Interest rates are comparable to those of short-term bonds.

Convertible Issues: See chapter 16.

Call Provisions: This permits the issuer to recall the bond when payments are no longer in their favor, and almost certainly will not favor the investor. Non-callable bonds are advised.

Straight (Non-convertible) Preferred Stocks

These should only be bought when available at bargain prices as the company may withhold payment at their discretion without any recourse. If the company has the ability to withhold dividend payments and does not have an obligation to repay them, it will be referred to as a non-cumulative security. These are the issues of which you need to be extremely wary.

Security Forms

These are among the many other types of financial instruments issued. Their advantage to the investor and the company lies in the fact that they are based on income tax provisions that are variable in both time and location. They are not for the uninformed investor.

CHAPTER 5
THE DEFENSIVE INVESTOR
AND COMMON STOCKS

CHAPTER SUMMARY

This chapter outlines four rules for the defensive investor with regard to picking common stock, where the common denominator is conservative measures. Graham also takes time to discuss growth stocks, suggesting that the defensive investor exercise caution. Further, he introduces three different personal backgrounds and explains how these are related to the investment object of choice. The concept of risk is also examined, and he explains why it is often misinterpreted.

CHAPTER OUTLINE

Investment Merits of Common Stocks

When the book was first written in 1949, common stocks had a bad reputation and the author went to lengths to persuade the reader that these stocks should still be included in an investor's portfolio. With the passage of twenty years, the reverse had occurred: the success of stocks had led to an illusion of safety—Graham points to the crash of 1929 and the quarter-century it took to recover from that. Stocks after 1957 lost their traditional advantage over the interest rate of bonds due to high prices and reduced dividend yield. The author had "no enthusiasm" for stocks when the DJIA was at 900 in 1971 and implies that a defensive position was warranted.

Rules for the Common Stock Component

The author suggests adhering to four rules:

1. Adequate diversification—somewhere between ten and thirty different issues.
2. Select large, prominent, conservatively financed companies.

3. Companies should have a long (twenty-plus years) unbroken record of dividend payment.

4. A seven-year price-to-earnings ratio (P/E) of less than twenty-five (less than twenty in the last twelve months); acknowledges this would eliminate the most popular companies on the DJIA and all so-called "growth" stocks.

Growth Stocks and the Defensive Investor

A growth stock has significantly exceeded the average on the market in its per-share earnings, and will double them in ten years. Since growth stocks sell at high multiples to their earnings, they introduce a speculative element. Graham notes that "Even the best of common stocks" lost 50% when the market turned down in '61-'62 and again in '69-'70.

For the reasons cited, growth stocks are considered too risky for the defensive investor. Large, currently unpopular, companies are unspectacular but may be a better bargain in the long run.

Portfolio Changes

As part of their services, brokers will perform a portfolio analysis. It is recommended that this review be performed at least annually by an appropriate selection of advisers.

Dollar Cost Averaging

This is the term used for investing the same amount of money in the same stock at fixed intervals, without any variation. Statistical analysis of all components of the DJIA over twenty-three periods of ten years showed an average profit of 21.5%.

Investor's Personal Situation

Three examples of different personal backgrounds are examined:

1. *A widow with children, who has a fixed inherited sum of money*: A conservative investment is essential; a mix of US Government bonds and the highest-quality stocks; stocks component might be as high as 75% if the market was advantageous. She definitely must not speculate.

2. *A doctor in mid-career with sizeable savings and continuing*

earnings: Unless he is willing to devote time to his investments, he also should accept the defensive investor role. Due perhaps to lack of time to look after their personal affairs, members of the medical profession are notoriously unsuccessful in the stock market. There may also be an inappropriate level of self-confidence in a field they do not understand and about which they are not willing to make the effort to learn.

3. *A young man with modest earnings and a capacity to save*: Some savings should go to Series E bonds; the balance should follow the standard for defensive investment.

The beginner in investments, who takes it seriously and wishes to learn, is urged not to try to "beat the market," but to concentrate on "price versus value" and to learn through experience, by investing small sums.

The securities to be purchased are less dependent on financial resources than they are on knowledge of finance, temperament and accumulated experience.

Note on the Concept of "Risk"

The terms "risk" and "safety," as used for securities, may be used in different senses, which may cause confusion.

The terms should be applied to the instrument that is bought, not to the investor (or speculator) who buys them. A US Government bond is essentially risk-free, whereas other bonds may be considered unsafe if they default on payments. The term "risk" is not applied to an individual stock or bond issue when it is part of a cyclical decline of the whole market; the owner is not obliged by the decline to sell and has not sustained a loss.

Note on "Large, Prominent and Conservatively Financed Corporations"

This term is used in describing the type of stock the conservative investor should acquire. Such a company is long established as a leader in its field, and in terms of size should be at least in the first third or quarter. The terms are used more as a guide than as an absolute measure.

CHAPTER 6
PORTFOLIO POLICY FOR
THE ENTERPRISING INVESTOR:
NEGATIVE APPROACH

CHAPTER SUMMARY

In this chapter, the focus changes to the enterprising investor, and focuses mainly on what he should *not* do. Five criteria are outlined, the common denominator of which is caution about anything that is not a proven high-quality security. Less-than-top-quality securities should only be purchased at bargain prices.

CHAPTER OUTLINE

The enterprising (more aggressive) investor should start his portfolio on the same basis as the conservative investor, with a mix of high-grade bonds and high-grade common stocks. From that base he will acquire other securities, but will always have a well-reasoned approach to their purchase.

The advice given by Graham is largely on the basis of what the enterprising investor should **NOT** do:

Leave high-grade preferred stocks to the corporate buyers;

Avoid inferior bonds and preferred stocks, except at bargain purchase levels;

Avoid foreign government bonds, despite the high yields offered;

Be wary of new issues;

Avoid common stocks with excellent, but only recent, earnings.

The choice of purchase of bonds should be the same as for the defensive investor.

Second-Grade Bonds and Preferred Stocks

In 1971, the yield on first-rate corporate bonds was 7.25%, so the purchase of second-grade issues for the same yield made no sense.

Companies without a strong credit rating had taken to the sale of "convertible bonds" that had warrants attached. This resulted in a situation where the bonds of second-grade companies issued without warrants (non-convertibles) were selling at a marked discount and might become suitable for purchase. The state of the market at the time Graham wrote, however, did not really support this, since less risky—but nearly as valuable—opportunities were freely available.

Although many investors buy bonds in order to obtain an income, and are tempted to buy inferior bonds because the income they offer is higher, it has historically proven unwise to follow this course for these are the bonds most likely to suspend payments when the market turns down, and most likely to lose face value. An example is quoted of railway bonds whose face value dropped from 102 to 68 in 1947. Despite the railways enjoying good earnings, the drop was due to a general downturn in the market. The bonds had been bought for a slightly better yield than that offered by government equivalents, but the ultimate loss in value was greater than experienced on the DJIA. It is bad business to accept the known possibility of a major loss of principal (basic amount invested) in exchange for 1-2% improvement in yearly income. Such a decision could only be justified if the bond was selling at a marked discount, but never justifiable if a premium was paid.

Second-grade bonds are liable, when the market turns down, to show a greater loss of face value than their better counterparts; however, when the market recovers, most of these bonds will also recover. Investors who take advantage of this swing in value will do very well.

It is common sense to refrain from buying securities at 100 when the experience of the market has shown they will be sold at 70 in the next market downturn.

Foreign Government Bonds

Two world wars and a major depression did not improve the reputation of foreign government bonds. Graham states that he has no concrete reason to suspect the future behavior of foreign government bonds, citing Australia and Norway as apparently stable countries, but nevertheless points to Cuba whose bonds fell to twenty cents on the dollar, and to the similar collapse of the bonds of Greece and Poland. He also adds a suggestion that Americans might choose to invest in their own country rather than a foreign one.

New Issues Generally

All investors should be wary of new issues, in part because they have salesmanship sponsoring, which needs to be met with a measure of sales resistance, and in part because the market conditions for new offers are chosen when they favor the seller (issuer) and must therefore not favor the buyer.

When the market swings up (bull market), privately owned companies tend to go public with sales of shares; when the market inevitably turns down, these tend to be hurt the most.

New Common-Stock Offerings

Newly issued shares may be issued on behalf of either an established company or a formerly private company now going public. Of necessity, the latter tend to be small operations with an inherent greater risk involved in buying their shares; they are launched when the market is on an upswing and may not survive a downswing. Graham points to an indicator of when the reverse is likely to occur: new common stocks of small companies are offered at prices higher than those of their established major counterparts and may later lose 75% of their selling price, often ending up below their true value.

It is bad policy to get mixed up in this sort of business. For every dollar you make, you will be lucky to lose only two. They may, however, prove excellent buys a few years later when nobody wants them and they are sold at a fraction of their true value.

CHAPTER 7
PORTFOLIO POLICY
FOR THE ENTERPRISING INVESTOR:
THE POSITIVE SIDE

CHAPTER SUMMARY

This chapter presents situations in which the enterprising investor enters the market for stocks and bonds. Further, it is explained that high returns can be made by entering large companies priced at less than net asset value (or book value). Companies that are not leaders in their industry can also be considered at bargain prices. Finally, the chapter concludes with the idea that the reader must choose to be either enterprising or defensive—there is no middle ground.

CHAPTER OUTLINE

Operations in Common Stocks
The enterprising investor will:
1. Buy low and sell high
2. Be careful with his selection
3. Buy extremely cheap picks
4. Buy securities with special situations.

General Market Policy – Formula Timing
Although it is an attractive notion to enter a depressed market and sell out at its peak, the special talent needed to sense this timing does not apply to the average investor for whom Graham is writing, and he therefore puts this notion aside. Although there may at one time have been a workable formula for increasing the proportion of stocks held according to market behavior, Graham believes no such formula exists anymore.

Growth Stock Approach

A growth stock is defined as one that has outperformed the market average and is expected to continue to outperform. Although it may seem obvious to concentrate on growth stocks, the matter is complicated, for the following reasons:

1. Stocks with good records and good prospects sell at high prices.
2. The investor's judgment of future opportunities may be incorrect. Unusually rapid growth is unlikely to last forever, and may in fact reverse.

It is possible to find examples of growth stocks that support any positive or negative argument put forward. An examination of forty-five funds specializing in growth stocks showed, however, that in one ten-year period they averaged a gain of 108%, while in the same decade the broad Standard & Poor's index of 500 stocks gained 105% and the narrower Dow Jones gained 83%. During the following two years, the majority of growth stock funds did worse than both the S&P and the DJIA.

The conclusion drawn from this is that the average investor who picks growth stocks is not likely to outperform the professional who manages the funds; therefore, no advantage is to be gained.

As a class, growth stocks tend to have wide swings in market price—even the largest of them such as GE and IBM—due to the influence of speculators indicating the potential for higher risk, which is proportionate with the rate of price rise.

Although Graham concedes large fortunes have been made from such growth stocks, he points out that these are mostly held by an individual with a close relationship to a single company into which he has invested all he owns. The average investor, lacking that relationship and impetus, is less likely to be as successful.

Three Recommended Fields for "Enterprising Investment"

To obtain better-than-average results, you must:

1. Have a plan that has rules and it's reasonably executed
2. Go against the crowd of other investors

To these ends, three different approaches are recommended:

The Relatively Unpopular Large Company

The market undervalues, in relative terms, companies that are neither showing growth nor are glamorous. The investor may concentrate on larger companies that are currently out of favor; such companies are well run and well resourced to the extent they can respond speedily to improvement.

This thesis was tried by examining the behavior of the most unpopular and cheapest stocks (determined by the previous year's P/E ratio) at the bottom of the DJIA, in the event anyone chose to invest in them, during a fifty-three-year period. From 1917-1933, this was not profitable. From 1937-1969, three of the cheap stocks underperformed, six equally performed and twenty-five outperformed the DJ index. It was computed that an investment between 1936 and 1962 in the stocks at the bottom of the DJ (with respect to low P/E ratios) would have raised $10,000 to $66,900. The same investment in the upper bracket stocks would have increased only to $25,300, and for the entire index list of stocks, $44,000. Further analysis between the years of 1968 and 1971 did not support the thesis, but Graham did not consider it should be abandoned.

Caution must be exercised in selecting from the list of lowest-price stocks (i.e., picking a stock simply because it has a low P/E ratio), since the occasional but recognizable anomalous situation may occur (for example, the company's future earnings forecast is negative).

Purchase of Bargain Issues

These are stocks or bonds which, all facts considered, appear to be selling below their real value. They are thought to be a bargain only if the indicated value is at least 50% greater than the selling price.

Such a decision is based on estimation of true value, which is calculated by considering anticipated future earnings and multiplying these by the factor used for the particular industry. There is also a question of the value of the business and its realizable assets to a private owner.

Such bargains are most commonly found at the low points of market swings when the "wisdom of having courage in depressed markets" comes into its own. The market also tends to "make mountains out of molehills," exaggerating minor problems and thereby creating opportunities in currently disappointing results.

But "currently disappointing" can only be determined in hindsight, and the investor should ensure the company has had stable earnings in the previous ten years and has the capacity in terms of finances and management to recover.

The stock of some companies may fall below the value of the company's assets. In 1957, 150 such companies were identified; over a two-year period, the price of such stocks rose 75% compared with a 50% gain in the whole S&P index, and none of them showed a loss. Such opportunities have become harder to find, but do still exist.

Bargain Issue Pattern in Secondary Companies

A "secondary company" is defined as a company that is not a leader in an important industry. Because of the experience of poor performance relative to the leaders in the 1931-1932 market downturn, secondary companies are less favored and sell at relatively lower prices, in some instances justifying the concept of a "bargain."

It should be remembered that these middle-sized companies, although not the leaders, are in fact large compared with privately held companies and there is no sound reason why they would not continue in business, earning a fair return on their capital.

In the post-World War II era, smaller companies did well, whereas the DJIA (representing large companies) rose 40% from 1938 to 1946. The S&P (representing less large companies) rose 280% which came to represent overvaluation of this group. This occurred again from 1961-1968 with new-concept companies representing electronics, computers and franchises. Then they were hit in the general decline, some to the point of undervaluation.

Reasons for which an undervalued stock might be selected for purchase:

1. A high dividend
2. Retained earnings is high
3. They perform well in a bull market
4. A new management may help the stock
5. Large companies may buy-out the pick

Bargain opportunities in bonds are more complex and less readily found.

Special Situations or "Workouts"

Large companies may buy smaller companies in the same field or in another field to expand their activities; they usually offer above market price to obtain the shares of the smaller company.

The market tends to undervalue the stock of any company involved in legal proceedings—"Never buy into a lawsuit," as the saying goes. This may offer opportunities to the informed speculator but not to most enterprising investors and never to the cautious investor.

Broader Implications of Our Rules for Investment

There is no room for a middle ground—the investor must either be passive or aggressive. Should he choose to be aggressive, that is enterprising; he must develop knowledge of security values, making his holdings in effect a business enterprise. Any compromise between these extremes will produce disappointment. You cannot be "half a businessman" and expect a half return. From this dictum, it follows that most investors should follow the passive route and accept the excellent returns of a defensive portfolio. For the investor, the three requirements are underlying safety, simplicity of choice and promise of satisfactory results. He will avoid anything exotic or complicated.

On the other hand, the enterprising investor may look into the purchase of anything he has adequate training on. He will avoid purchasing at full price (close to par) foreign bonds, ordinary preferred stocks, secondary common stocks and original offerings, but may buy them at bargain prices—not more than two-thirds of the appraised value.

Financial history shows that the investor may only expect satisfactory results from secondary stocks when they are bought at bargain prices. Exceptions may be made for stocks that lie in a border range between big and small, and for them the margin of "bargain" may be lessened.

CHAPTER 8
THE INVESTOR AND MARKET FLUCTUATIONS

CHAPTER SUMMARY

This chapter outlines why the intelligent investor should welcome and benefit from market fluctuations. He does this by focusing on the difference between the price and value of a security. To exemplify, Graham advises caution regarding timing the stock market, and provides a summary of the historical characteristics of a bull market. An investor can protect himself from engaging negatively in market fluctuations only by entering stocks with sound fundamentals. One example given is not paying a price higher than 1.33 times the book value.

Further, it is argued that, when it comes to the highs and lows of market fluctuations, the investor should solely observe, not react to the market price when already invested. Benjamin Graham sees investors as business partners. A business partner would not expect to get a new partner or a price quote every day. With regard to bonds, it is concluded that price cannot be predicted; however, depending on the investor's requirements, the size of price fluctuations can be anticipated between categories of bonds.

CHAPTER OUTLINE

The investor should be aware of the probability of price swings, and should be prepared for them financially and psychologically. US Government bonds will not lose their face value in any market; high-grade bonds with a short term of seven years or fewer will show less change in price due to market swings than can be expected of long-term bonds, and common stock value will certainly be affected by market ups and downs.

These swings tend to incite the investor to speculate, and although it is easy to say, "Do not speculate" it is not always easy for the investor to follow that advice. Graham modifies his, "Do not speculate" to, "If you want to speculate, do so with your eyes open, knowing that you will probably lose money in the end. Be sure to limit the amount at risk; separate it completely from your investment program."

Market Fluctuations as a Guide to Investment Decisions

The intelligent investor should be prepared to **profit** from the inevitable swings in market values, and may do this either by *timing* or by *pricing*. "Timing" is an anticipation of market changes. "Pricing" is the same as buy low and sell high, or, at the very least, make sure you are not buying at the high extreme of the market's swing.

The intelligent investor will benefit from "pricing," whereas the investor who practices "timing" will become a speculator. Graham makes his negative views plain with regard to the ability to forecast the market, and those who would have you believe they can: "It is absurd to think that the general public can ever make money out of market forecasts."

Timing is of great psychological importance to the speculator who wants to make his money in a hurry, whereas the investor is prepared to wait patiently for the appropriate opportunity; for him, "timing" must coincide with "pricing."

A mechanism known as the "Dow theory" purported to give a signal for timing purchases. If this was ever valid, it lost its value when all traders were aware of it and followed it, and hindsight has shown that the trader who just stayed in the market with a DJIA portfolio fared better than the ones who went in and out following the timing indications of the Dow theory. Graham explains that theories can be made to look good when adapted with hindsight, but lose their value when commonly accepted and employed.

"Buy Low – Sell High" Approach

The average investor cannot expect to forecast price movements, so the question arises as to whether he can benefit from the movement after it has occurred? The classic description of a "shrewd investor" is one who did just that by buying in a bear market and selling in a bull market, doing the opposite to what other investors (and speculators) were doing.

Looking at market cycles between 1897 and 1949, this included ten complete cycles; six were over within four years; four ran for six to seven years; one for eleven years (1921-32). The swing in prices from low to high (advances) varied between 44% and 500%, with most between 50% and 100%; subsequent declines varied from 24% to 89%, with most in the 40% to 50% range, but a 50% decline fully offset a previous 100% advance.

Nearly all bull markets were characterized by the following:

1. Historically high price level.
2. High price/earnings ratio (P/E).
3. Low dividend yields as against bond yields.
4. Much speculation on margin.
5. Many new common stock issues of low quality.

With hindsight, it would appear possible to have benefitted from the "buy low and sell high" dictum, but in fact multiple minor variations in major swings frustrated such an attempt. Graham therefore modified his advice, suggesting buying and altering the *proportion* of the investment in stocks and bonds at what seems a favorable moment in the cycle, as it can best be interpreted in real time; i.e., as the investor is actually experiencing it, without the benefit of hindsight.

Formula Plans

It is easy to devise a formula that both sounds logical and can be made to show what would have happened had it been applied to the historical record. One such formula is an automatic selling of some stock with substantial rises in the market, which, if followed, would leave the investor holding no stock after a substantial rise. Those who followed this formula in the 1950s found themselves with empty portfolios in a market that continued to advance, but prices were now too high to re-enter it.

In the market, any approach to making money that is readily described and followed is, by its very nature, too simple and too easy to last.

Market Fluctuations of the Investor's Portfolio

Investors must expect to see fluctuations in the value of their stocks. The shares of secondary companies are liable to experience a wider fluctuation than those of the primary, larger, companies. The investor must accept that in any five-year period his stocks may advance 50% only to fall back 33%, and must understand that fluctuations in listed prices on the exchange neither make him richer nor poorer.

A substantial rise in the market may provoke an imprudent reaction. Should the investor now sell? Or should he behave like the general public; i.e., be overconfident, and buy more? The question is framed by Graham to ensure his reader rejects the second option, but he states that, because of the frailty of human nature, a mechanism to guard against temptation and the urge "to do something" should be in place. The suggestion is that, as the market advances, part of the new more highly valued stock portfolio should be sold and the revenue invested in bonds. The reverse process would be followed in a declining market.

- I would like to highlight that Graham fails to discuss the implication of paying capital gains during this type of movement from stocks to bonds or vice versa. This is a very important consideration as you assess the potential return of the new security.

Business Valuations versus Stock Market Valuations

There may be a marked difference between the total value of a company's shares and the actual value of the company itself. "Book value," also known as "net asset value" and "balance sheet value" is what a company would be worth if sold for its physical and financial assets. The cumulative value of the company's shares is likely to trade substantially greater than its book value, and the more successful the company becomes, the wider the difference will become between book value and market (share) price. Put another way, the more successful the company, the greater the element of speculation in its shares becomes, which explains why there may be marked fluctuation in share value of the most successful companies. IBM and Xerox are given as examples.

Taking the element of speculation into consideration, Graham recommends not buying a stock when the market valuation, the speculative premium, exceeds book value by more than a third. Therefore the P/BV ratio should not exceed 1.33. Stocks whose market value is close to book value are not necessarily a good buy; the investor should ensure there is also a satisfactory price-to-earnings ratio (P/E), and a sound financial position with a good prospect of long-term earnings. Such stocks are less likely to be affected by market fluctuations since there is a smaller "speculative premium" in their market price. Graham found at the time he was writing that there were many good-quality opportunities on the DJIA that met these criteria.

The A&P Example

In full, the company known loosely and widely as "A&P" is the "Great Atlantic & Pacific Tea Co." In 1929, when first launched, the shares sold at $494. Then the slump came, and in 1932 the shares of the successful company fell to $104; in 1936 they sold between 111 and 131; after the recession of 1938, they fell to $36. Although A&P at the time was perhaps the largest retailer in the world, the market in 1938 valued it at less than its very substantial book value, largely on the basis of fear of the Depression.

Speed and Reflections

In 1939, the shares had tripled in market value and were back to 117 (from the 1938 low); in 1961 (allowing for splitting of shares) the equivalent of market price was 705, and at thirty times the price-earnings ratio, whereas the average P/E ratio on the DJIA was twenty-three. The shares continued to fall markedly, and in 1972 A&P had a deficit.

Graham, from this example, points out a) how the stock market is often wrong, thereby providing opportunities for an, "Alert and courageous investor," and b) how businesses may improve or deteriorate in efficiency over a period of time, and the investor must be aware of the company's performance.

An investor is virtually never obliged by the market to sell his shares; however, if he watches market price too closely and is influenced by fluctuations in price into making a decision that is contrary to the original plan, it would be better for him if he had remained ignorant of the price change. On a par with this misunderstanding is the investor who holds property for which there is no quoted valuation, and believes that because there is no change in a number there has been no change in market value.

To emphasize this point, an analogy is drawn between being a partner in a private business and holding shares in a public company. If every day another partner offered either to buy your share or sell you part of his, and every day his offer switched from the previous one, how would you assess his judgment? Equivalently, the investor should be aware of market prices, but should not let fluctuations concern him beyond a decision to buy wisely when prices have truly fallen, or to sell wisely when they have risen. Between these lows and highs, he should ignore the market price and watch, instead, the operations of the company and its declared dividends.

Summary

The speculator hopes to profit from market fluctuations. The investor buys and holds suitable securities at suitable prices; he concerns himself with price movements only so far as "lows and highs." Meanwhile, if the investor has the available funds, he will look for the ever-present bargain opportunities.

The investor should remember that market quotations are there for his convenience and may be ignored or heeded as he wishes. He should follow the axiom, "Never buy a stock immediately after a substantial rise nor sell one immediately after a substantial drop."

An Added Consideration

The managers of a company may declare they are not responsible for the market evaluation of their company or for variation in price. This may be true of daily minor fluctuations but is not true of the overall direction of market valuation. Good management results in a good average market price—and bad management the opposite.

Fluctuations in Bond Prices

The market price of long-term bonds responds to interest rates, given the inverse relationship between low yields and high prices—at least that is the general, but not invariable, rule. To this Graham draws a moral: "Nothing important on Wall Street (the term used for the stock and bond market) can be counted on to occur exactly in the same way as it happened before; however, the more it changes, the more it is the same thing."

Therefore, it is completely impossible to make predictions about the price of bonds; thus the investor must make his purchase in accordance with his requirements. If it is important that the market value will not decrease, he should buy US savings bonds, series E or H. If, however, he seeks the best interest rates, he should look to a selection of long-term corporate or tax-free municipal bonds, but must expect fluctuation in market price.

Convertible bonds have often been sold by companies with less-than-attractive credit ratings and often have wider-than-usual price fluctuations. Only a deluded investor could expect an ideal combination of high-grade bond and price protection, or even gain.

The investor has a choice in bonds between stability of price and low interest rate, or better fixed income with fluctuation in bond price. The ideal would be a combination of fixed price with a better interest rate—and the US savings bonds are the closest approximation to that ideal.

CHAPTER 9
INVESTING IN INVESTMENT FUNDS

CHAPTER SUMMARY

In this chapter, Benjamin Graham suggests that an average individual stock investor performs worse than an investor who puts his money into a mutual fund. It is argued that mutual funds in general perform close to the market, while the individual fund deviates widely from the market. The explanation for this may come down to speculation, and in any case past performance is no guarantee for the future. Even so, the best measure of performance is made during a recession. Lastly, closed-ended attributes and balanced funds are discussed.

CHAPTER OUTLINE

A corps of salesmen offers "mutual funds," also known as "open funds," which are redeemable at net asset value; non-redeemable equivalents are known as "closed funds" and their price varies, similar to that of listed stock. These funds are supervised by the Securities and Exchange Commission (SEC).

- Note: In 2002, there were (in the US) more than eight thousand funds handling more than six trillion invested dollars.

The various types of funds may be classified:

According to proportion of holdings; e.g., balanced funds maintain proportional holdings of bonds versus stocks.

According to objective; e.g., growth, or income, or price stability; some specialize in an area of the business economy such as chemicals, aviation, overseas stock, etc.

According to sales technique; "load funds" carry an up-front sales commission of as much as 9% merely to buy them; "no-load funds" do not, hence they are not popular with salesmen.

There are particular arrangements for taxation of interest, dividends and profits, which the investor ought to understand before committing himself to any purchase. The field is vast and can be confusing. He will want to know:

Is there a way he can obtain better-than-average results?

If not, how can he avoid worse-than-average results?

What type of fund should he choose?

Investment Fund Performance as a Whole

It is quite certain that funds have served a useful purpose. They have promoted the habit of saving and investing. They have protected the uninformed from mistakes they might have made if they had acted on their own initiative in the market. Their returns have kept pace with the market. Graham offers a guess that the "average investor" who put his money in mutual funds would have done better in a decade than the equivalent investor who picked his own stocks. But he says the real choice confronting the investor is between the man promoting funds and the one pushing low-grade stocks; the purchase of mutual funds is also a safeguard against the temptation to speculate.

To determine how well the funds performed, the performance of ten of the largest funds was examined over a period of ten years. On average, they matched or slightly outperformed the S&P 500 index, and substantially outperformed the DJIA. The explanation for the funds matching the index is that they are so large that in fact, "They *are* the market." A wide difference was found, however, between the performances of individual funds.

- Note: Current evidence points to the idea that most mutual funds perform worse than the DJIA.

An explanation as to why one fund does better than another may lie in the possibility that the manager has taken undue risks—in effect speculated, and *has gotten away with it for a while*. He may also just be a better manager. But his good fortune may not hold; past results do not guarantee future results, and management changes quite frequently.

"Performance" Funds

Although a perfectly legitimate intention, the managers of "performance funds" have set out to "beat the index." Their funds are usually small, and for a time they may succeed, but as the fund grows, their potential for beating the index declines. In many cases, the relatively young managers had worked only in a bull market when all stocks were doing well, and were prepared to take risks (i.e., speculate) in a manner that those with longer experience did not consider wise. An example is given in which a well-known fund placed its investors' money in two companies that promptly went bankrupt. Another profile is given of a named set of young managers whose funds did well for two years then fell below the index level: "Bright, energetic, young people have promised to perform miracles with other people's money since time began."

Fifty years ago, outright swindles on the market were rampant. With the formation of the SEC, the methods changed, but new methods of fooling the public were devised—but the urge to speculate is ever present.

The only way to judge a performance fund is to look at the record when it was not a boom year on the market, and/or discount that year from its reported performance. Those that continued to show growth were all small, suggesting size is critical to performance in an inverse manner.

Closed-End versus Open-End Funds

Closed-end funds, mostly older on the market than the open-end funds, have a fixed capital value and are sold to a much lesser degree. They do not have salesmen promoting them, unlike their counterparts of the open ends.

The open-end fund price, if "front-loaded" carries an immediate high commission to the salesman, whereas the closed-end fund, like a bond, may be sold for less than face value. For these reasons, Graham suggests it is better to buy a closed-end fund at a 10-15% discount than an open-end fund with a 9% sales fee. If the performance of the two funds is the same (they would have to hold similar stock) it is obvious the closed-end fund is a better buy. The benefit is less obvious if compared with a "no-load" mutual fund that has the advantage that it can always (or nearly always!) be cashed in for market value without a discount.

There are closed-end funds that sell on the market at a premium, but an examination of the potential benefits would not recommend these to investors.

Investment in Balanced Funds

A balanced fund is one that has stock and bond components. An examination of twenty-three different balanced funds showed that an average of 40% of their capital was placed in bonds. The funds' average return on the offering price was 3.6%, which was less than the return of US savings bonds during that period.

CHAPTER 10
THE INVESTOR AND HIS ADVISERS

CHAPTER SUMMARY

In this chapter, Graham argues that the more an investor relies on advice from others, the more conservative his investment approach should be. Advice can come from different sources and at different costs; however, the intelligent investor must base his decisions on a wider range of factors. While brokers may have high integrity, their pay is based on commission sales, which can lead to advice that encourages the investor to speculate. Furthermore, it is outlined that the average investor should not expect better-than-average returns from listening to advisers. The enterprising investor may benefit more from advisors, as he is able to evaluate the potential pick further.

CHAPTER OUTLINE

The investment of money is unique in the business world because it is almost always based on advice from others. In effect, the investor is asking some other person to tell him how to make money, whereas if a businessman seeks advice it will be on the direction of some aspect of his business, not simply on, "How can I make a profit?" The situation becomes particularly strange when the investor requires (or the adviser offers) better-than-average returns.

Such advice may come from a non-professional friend or relation, your banker, an investment broker, financial service or counselor, or even a financial paper or magazine. Graham's advice is: "If the investor must rely on the advice of other persons, he should limit himself strictly to conservative and unimaginative investments."

Investment Counsel and Trust Services of Banks

The leading investment counsel firms, trust firms and banks do not claim to be brilliant, but they do claim to be careful and competent, which means they should at a minimum preserve your capital. Their chief value lies in preventing their clients from themselves—i.e., from making costly mistakes—and typically they are engaged by people who do not wish to look after the boring details of their wealth.

Financial Services

The cost of such services is less than that of investment counselors. Their clients are investors (or speculators) who want a "hands-on" attitude to the money they have (or would like to have). Some financial services produce highly technical reports on market activity and do not give direct investment advice. Some of them make market forecasts, usually phrased and hedged so cautiously that they can claim to have been right in their prediction no matter what actually happens—the same meaningless phrases occur over and over. There is a demand for being told what will happen, and these "experts" merely respond to that demand.

Graham makes a general criticism of their commonly given advice: that it recommends purchase or sale of stock on the near-term prospects without paying attention to current price, in such a manner that no attempt is made to determine if the stock is overvalued or undervalued.

The intelligent investor may take notice of the information offered, and even of suggestions, but will base his investment decisions on a wider range of factors.

Advice from Brokerage Houses

The largest volume of information comes from stockbrokers and is distributed to their clients on a regular, no-charge basis. Graham expresses a view that, in general, the brokers thrive on speculation, and their advice therefore must always be suspect. He also says that some act only in a responsive manner, providing information when asked and carrying out orders as requested, but do not induce sales or encourage speculation. Some, he feels, will, "Give the customer what they want," and will cater to speculators' urges, suffering in order just to be busy on the market—an attitude Graham is convinced will lead to losses.

Although he concedes the broker is an honorable man and follows a rigid code of conduct, Graham is convinced that, because the broker makes commissions on his sales, he must of necessity encourage his clients (some would say "customers") to speculate. He will not, however, be insensitive to being told speculation is not this investor's wish.

A financial (securities) analyst has a different role: he investigates and analyses the stock, reports on it—but does not sell it. Although anyone can call himself a financial analyst, the profession has a diploma, Chartered Financial Analyst (CFA), which requires very real study and experience before it is awarded. That does not mean the advice of a CFA must necessarily be followed, however. The value of the analyst to the investor depends on the investor himself. His function is to give information about a stock; he should not be expected to assume the broker's role and give advice as to whether to buy or sell. In general, the average investor will not have access to the brokerage-house analyst.

The CFA Certificate for Financial Analysts

This diploma was created in 1963, after twenty years of urging by Graham, with the intention of it being comparable to the title of Certified Public Accountant. Apart from wishing to establish a set program of required training, it was also the intention to raise public esteem to the level of considering the analyst a "professional," a nebulous concept not always held of the broker.

Dealings with Brokerage Houses

Although the officers who control the stock exchanges have a stern code of conduct and demanding financial criteria, some brokerage houses occasionally face insolvency, and may or may not be bailed out by others in the industry. Although the excuses may vary from too many orders to too few, it is more likely that the failures were caused by the partners speculating (i.e. gambling) on the market in their own account, and using funds that were designated as an untouchable reserve.

Clearly the investor should deal only with a "reputable" broker. Unfortunately, however, some insolvencies have involved firms of high repute and long history. Graham recommended that the investor have his bank hold the paper securities.

- Note: In today's market, very few investors actually hold the paper; the records are kept electronically and fear of loss is minimized by the Securities Investor Protection Corporation (SIPC), a government-mandated consortium of brokers that, since 1970, has assured against any exchange losses.

The institutional buyer of stocks in large quantities is as well informed as the broker he deals with. The small investor, on the other hand, is not, and in his ignorance and naïveté is readily taken advantage of. As such, and it is not prudent for him to accept the recommendation of the broker with the same confidence he might give his priest or doctor; he should listen to the advice but bring to it his own judgment, or possibly even seek further advice elsewhere.

Other Advisers

The advice is, "Consult your banker." "Your accountant" could equally have been suggested. This is not because either will be an expert on investments, but because he will almost certainly be conservative by nature and will not favor speculating.

In terms of discussing investments with friends or relatives, "Much bad advice is given free."

Summary

Advice on investments is to be had for a fee from an investment counselor, or without charge from a brokerage house. The investor should not expect better-than-average results and should be extremely wary of anyone who promises spectacular ones.

The defensive investor will know he is not qualified to judge the value of the pieces of advice he is given. He should, however, be crystal clear about his objectives and the type of advice he wishes to have—that is to say, high-grade bonds and the stocks of leading companies, and not at prices at the top of their market

On the other hand, the aggressive, enterprising investor will want the full details of the advice he is given, and will use his own (modestly informed) judgment on whether to follow it. Not until his securities adviser has proved his value over a significant period of time will the investor accept his advice blindly.

CHAPTER 11
SECURITY ANALYSIS
FOR THE LAY INVESTOR:
GENERAL APPROACH

CHAPTER SUMMARY

In this chapter, the work of a security analyst is examined. While the analyst should be able to interpret the financial results, he should not be tempted to use advanced math for common stock. For bond analysis, Graham gives a rule of thumb that the EPS should be three times the per-share fixed obligations of the company, among other recommendations. For common stock analysis, capitalization and discount rate are introduced as a means by which to compare and equate current price with an estimate of future earnings. For estimating the capitalization rate, four key determinants are considered.

A formula for valuing growth stocks is also presented; however, Benjamin Graham himself is reluctant to place much trust in the method. The same undependability applies to detailed industry reports, which it is up to the individual investor to evaluate.

CHAPTER OUTLINE

Financial analysis has become a well-established profession, with a set code of ethics, associations and professional journals, each with their own set of unresolved problems.

The earlier term, "security analysis," was deliberately limiting in concept to an analyst who dealt with the past, present and future of any given security issue. Although it has tended to be replaced by the wider concept of "financial analyst," for the purpose of his book Graham preferred to rest with "security analyst."

In his report, the security analyst would describe the business under consideration: its operating and financial results, strong and weak points, potential for future earnings, comparisons with like companies in the same industry. He would then render an opinion based on his findings in regard to both safety and attractiveness of purchase of bond or stock.

The security analyst must be able to read between the lines of the accountants' reports and recognize items that have been passed over. He will establish guides to safety of purchase based on past earnings, capital structure, working capital, asset values and other items he finds to be significant in forming an opinion. Analysis of "growth stocks," which lack a historical track record, is important but more difficult. This has given rise to complicated mathematical techniques purported to enhance the validity of the opinion offered, and these are most likely to occur at the occasions when they can be considered least reliable. This requirement of the industry has, however, propelled the security analyst into the realm of mathematics and pseudo-science.

But Graham—forty-four years of experience in the industry and a founder of the specialty—says, "I have never seen dependable calculations made about common stock values that went beyond simple arithmetic or the most elementary algebra. Whenever calculus is brought in, or higher algebra, you could take it as a warning signal that the operator was trying to substitute theory for experience, and usually also to give speculation the deceptive guise of investment."

It is appropriate for the investor to understand what the security analyst is saying, and to distinguish between sound analysis and the merely superficial. This will begin with the interpretation of the company's annual financial report.

Bond Analysis

This is the most dependable (most respected) branch of security analysis, and relates to determination of safety—i.e., quality—of bond issues.

The chief criterion applied is the number of times in the past that total interest charges have been covered by available earnings. For preferred stocks, the criterion is applied to combined bond interest and preferred dividends. Graham states, however, that the tests are somewhat arbitrary and standards vary between analysts. He applies his own test to *average* results over seven years, whereas other analysts might require a *minimum* coverage for every year in the timeframe considered. Graham concedes a *poorest year* as an alternative to the seven-year average, which could be set at two-thirds of the seven-year requirement.

Generally speaking, the net income of a business should exceed the fixed income expenses of a business by at least three times in order to be considered desirable. In the book, Graham provides a chart based on type of enterprise, comparing them before and after taxes. Since the list of enterprises is limited in scope—and out of date—I have prescribed a rule of thumb (from the chart) that the EPS should be three times the per-share fixed obligations of the company.

In addition to this recommendation, the following are some of the other tests Graham recommends:

1. *Size of Enterprise:* Consideration must be given to the size of the business and its ability to flex resources in order to meet payments

2. *Stock/Equity Ratio:* Ratio between market price of common stock and the total debt. This has the double benefit of determining whether the company could withstand an unexpected adverse development, and ascertaining the opinion the market holds of the company.

3. *Property Value:* Asset values revealed on the balance sheet were at one time considered the chief security for a bond issue; however, it is now thought that safety is in earnings power, without which the assets are liable to lose their reported value.

Evaluation of tests of safety can only be achieved in hindsight, but the bonds and preferred stocks of the corporations that have met the stringent tests described have continued to be safe. On the other side of the coin, companies that went bankrupt, for instance railroads, were signaled by these tests as unsafe for investment. Those railroads that did not end in bankruptcy did pass the tests, and in the instance cited of the Penn Central Railroad, the inadequacy to meet standards was signaled to the prudent investor long before its eventual collapse.

Public utilities have received the particular attention of the SEC since the disasters of the 1930s, and bankruptcies in that field are now unknown.

Long-term industrial bonds have not always fared as well; there has been less stability. The recommendation made is that the investor should purchase only the bonds and preferred stocks of companies of sufficient size because they could withstand a depression. It should be noted, however, that, at the time of writing, in the period when there had been no depression there had been a considerable expansion of long-term debt producing operating losses, and "over-bonded" companies had become all too familiar.

Common Stock Analysis

Analysis requires comparing current price with an estimate of future earnings multiplied by an appropriate "capitalization factor."

- Note: The terms "capitalization factor" and "discount rate" are very similar terminology. Here's the difference: if you've ever worked in real estate valuation, you'll often hear the term "cap rate." The cap rate is used to equate potential operating income to value. In this context, operating income is the difference between estimated revenues and estimated expenses of the present business model. That number is multiplied by a fixed ratio to determine a value. In real estate, the cap rate typically varies according to each geographical area. A discount rate, on the other hand, takes the process one step further. In addition to valuing current operating income, it accounts for a future income and earnings growth. It takes those earnings estimates and "discounts" the future cash flow back to the present value. Warren Buffett prescribes to the use of a discount rate. To many, these terms are used interchangeably. An easy way to determine which term is more accurate is to think of it in these terms: if earnings are expected to remain constant, a cap rate/ cap factor is probably the correct terminology; if earnings are expected to increase or decrease over time, a discount rate is most likely a more appropriate term to use.

This estimate must start with historical data of physical volume, prices received and operating margin, from which future sales may be projected. Such a projection requires consideration of the general economic forecasts of gross national product (GNP) and then those forecasts specific to the industry in question. Based on the historical records of companies that conducted these analyses, some of which were correct and others not, Graham concludes that an estimate of the performance of a group is more likely to be correct than that of the performance of an individual company.

Ideally, the analyst will pick for his client the small number of companies he knows best from within this group, and that he believes are most likely to succeed; however, in practice, analysts seem to have failed to be able to do this. So the practical fund managers diversify their stock, accepting that some will do better than others but that the best will be among them. By practicing diversification, the managers implicitly state that they do not believe in the myth of "selectivity." And, again, in practice, the funds that chose the supposedly best in a group have not outperformed those that invested in the group as a whole.

- Note: This statement by Benjamin Graham was unquestionably proved wrong by his star pupil—Warren Buffett.

Factors Affecting the Capitalization Rate

Average future earnings are supposed to be the chief determinant of value, but are not the only criterion the analyst will depend on; he also investigates other factors to determine a "capitalization rate."

1. *General Long-Term Prospects:* Although no one can forecast the future, it falls to the analyst to attempt to do so. And price/earnings ratio (P/E) is one of the tools to measure both an industry and an individual company within an industry, thus giving credence to the belief that the market is often correct, except when past performance is the only factor considered. In this regard, Graham cites an instance when the chemicals industry was incorrectly supposed to outperform the oil companies. This is one of many easily found occasions when the expert forecasters of the market (colloquially known as "Wall Street") were wrong.

2. *Management:* Although not open to clear analysis, but it is easy to suppose successful companies are well managed, and vice versa. To take management into consideration may exaggerate its role in a company's success, but it should be noted when there has been a recent change. He cites two occasions when Chrysler Motors was "rescued" by new management.

3. *Financial Strength and Capital Structure:* The stock in a well-financed company is clearly a better buy at a given price than stock in a company with a heavy debt load.

4. *Dividend Record:* Uninterrupted dividend payments for as long as twenty years weigh heavily in a company's favor. The standard dividend policy followed by most companies and known as the "dividend payout ratio" was (at the time the book was written) to pay out two-thirds of average earnings in dividends. Since that time, as a result of changes in tax laws, the ratio has fallen as low as 25%. Other corporations have chosen to employ profits to expand their business rather than pay out dividends.

Capitalization Rates for Growth Stocks

Graham offers a more simple formula for appraising the value of a growth stock:

Value = Current (Normal) Earnings x (8.5 plus twice the expected annual growth rate)

where the growth figure is that expected over the next seven to ten years. Clearly such a formula could be extrapolated over time to give the company a value of infinity, so the analyst introduces a "margin of safety" in an assigned objective.

Graham applied his formula to a number of large companies. For two it proved valid; for four it did not—and he warns that forecasting the future does not have a high degree of reliability. Future values depend to an extent on future interest rates, and to forecast them, "Is almost presumptuous."

But Graham knows no better formula, for growth stocks specifically, than the one he offers.

Industry Analysis

It is logical to suppose that a company that leads in its segment of industry will do better than those that do not. To this end, detailed analyses of companies are made. There is, however, limited value for the investor in familiarizing himself with such studies, since they are widely known and already reflected in the market pricing—though Wall

Street's view of the future is remarkably fallible. Familiarization with new developments within a company might lead to an investment with great rewards in the future, or might be a total failure. Only the individual investor can decide which is right for him.

A Two-Part Appraisal Process

Graham gives the opinion that methods of appraisal of stock need to be changed.

In the two-part process, an appraisal is first made on past performance, and requires the assumption the world will remain unchanged for the next seven years; the second phase of the analysis is to determine what future conditions might alter this steady path.

This task requires the work of both senior and junior analysts working in sequence. The senior of the analysts would first create a formula to be applied to all companies' past performance; the junior would apply routine studies to the designated companies. The senior would then make a conclusion with regard to the probability of future performance differing from that of the past, and give the reasoning behind his conclusions.

Graham, a founder and leader in the profession of financial analysts, states, "We doubt whether the valuations thus reached will prove sufficiently dependable in the case of the typical industrial company, great or small.

But he does think the practice of forecasting is worth pursuing, for the following reasons:

a) Many analysts are obliged to do it anyway, and he thinks his method should be followed.

b) It will give experience to those who practice it.

c) Such work will create an invaluable background of recorded experience, which might be a foundation for improved procedures.

CHAPTER 12
THINGS TO CONSIDER ABOUT PER-SHARE EARNINGS

CHAPTER SUMMARY

This chapter explains how and why the investor should be cautious about earnings per share. Since they can be manipulated both higher and lower within accounting laws, an average earnings measure of seven to ten years is suggested, to provide a more realistic reflection of earnings. Finally, the chapter addresses the issue that, while it is important for an investor to determine the growth factor from a company's history, there is no definitive way of determining how many years should be included. Irrespective of the approach used, a more optimistic growth rate would also increase the risk of the investment.

CHAPTER OUTLINE

Here, the reader will find two pieces of seemingly contradictory advice:

Don't take a single year's earnings seriously.

If you do, watch for booby-traps in per-share figures.

Graham goes on to explain that "Earnings per share" cannot be taken at face value, and the footnotes must be read to find that, although primary earnings per share were reported at $5.20, net income after special charges was 4.32, and fully diluted after special charges was 4.19.

The "dilution factor" is an allowance for the potential of conversion of a bond issue into common shares.

Special charges carry vagueness and seem to be used at the discretion of management and accountants rather than on a fixed calendar basis. In the case cited (ALCOA), they were for anticipated costs of closing down divisions and plants and other estimated future costs. What some might consider sleight of hand is perfectly acceptable in accounting rules and allows the company to reduce its apparent earnings when they are good. Then, if the actual costs occur in a less successful year, they do not have to be shown, since they have already appeared on the books. In fact in that year, the delayed tax credit can be shown, boosting the earnings.

Alternatively, if everyone expects the year to have universal poor results, then that is the time for a company with earnings to write off future losses, because no one was expecting success. Graham expresses "Lingering doubts" about the decency of these ethically and legally accepted accounting and business practices.

A more open accounting practice was the "contingency reserve" whereby profits were put aside in order to even out future earnings. Accountants rejected this on the grounds that it hid the true earnings and that shareholders must know the truth of what was done by the company during the period reported. It is questionable whether this has happened to the satisfaction of anyone who is not an accountant.

To return to the change in reported earnings from 5.20 dropping to 4.19, Graham says the information provided did not permit an assessment of the true earnings for the year since it is mixed with so many "might happen" factors of the future.

The use of accounting "techniques" of this kind makes it extremely difficult even for the fully informed expert analyst to compare one company with another.

Three accounting rules described are: special charges, income tax benefits delayed, and dilution factor; a fourth is the choice of depreciation, either straight-line or accelerated, which can make a substantial difference to the reported earnings as well as confusing comparisons of earnings in years when different depreciation styles were employed.

A fifth choice the accountant has to make is whether research and development costs (R&D) should be charged as they occur or amortized over several years.

- Note: amortization is simply a fancy name for the depreciation of an intangible asset.

A sixth decision for the accountant's report is whether to value the inventory on the basis of first in, first out (FIFO) or last in, first out (LIFO).

A seventh is the ability of a company to generate paper losses from the sale of a division, then claim tax benefits from these losses against the earnings of its successful business, thereby apparently nullifying the earnings.

Many or most of these issues are of small significance, but the investor should be aware that they exist. And there are many other maneuvers accountants employ, which to them are ethical, and to the lawyers are legal—but to the investor are highly deceptive.

Use of Average Earnings

A "mean figure" for average earnings over a substantial time, seven to ten years, was thought to represent a company's earnings more realistically than the single yearly report. It does have the advantage of incorporating all the "special charges" and other items found in the footnotes.

Calculation of the Past Growth Rate

It is extremely important for an investor to understand and determine the growth factor from a company's history of business. Although an investor can simply use an average growth rate for long-term figures, it is suggested to use an average when short-term growth has been strong. If this is the case, investors should potentially look at the average growth rate from the last three years to the long-term growth rate of ten years. There is no way of definitively determining how many years should be included or excluded. This is where growth estimates become an art for the analyst. Regardless of the approach, estimates that lean towards a more optimistic outlook will most likely increase the risk of the investment.

CHAPTER 13
A COMPARISON OF
FOUR LISTED COMPANIES

CHAPTER SUMMARY

In this chapter, four random companies are analyzed using six comparison criteria. Benjamin Graham concludes with a comment on the attributes of the stocks he prefers from the different investing approaches. He also provides general observations about risks that are independent of the approach.

CHAPTER OUTLINE

This chapter is devoted to putting "security analysis" into practical exercise. For this purpose, four companies were selected at random from those listed on the New York Stock Exchange (NYSE): ELTRA, Emerson Electric, Emery Air Freight, and Emhart.

The data examined and tabulated comprised capitalization, income items, balance sheet items, ratios, and price record. They were examined in a comparative manner for:

1. Profitability: All companies showed satisfactory earnings on book value. Emerson and Emery were highest and it is noted that a high rate of return on capital is accompanied by a high annual growth rate. The profit per dollar of sales was satisfactory for all four companies, Emerson in particular.

2. Stability: Measured by the maximum decline in per-share earnings in any one of the previous ten years. No company showed total stability; ELTRA and Emhart showed the least decline in the bad year, with 8%, compared with the DJIA decline of 7%.

3. Growth: The two low-multiplier companies had satisfactory growth rates; the high-multiplier companies were (of course) better.

4. Financial Position: The three manufacturing companies were financially sound; Emery Air Freight was in a different category. All four companies had low long-term debt.

5. Dividends: The important factor is a history of uninterrupted payment of dividends; Emhart had paid dividends without fail since 1902; the other companies were newer but had no failed years.

6. Price History: All companies did very well over the 34-year period in comparison with the DJIA; in particular the air freight company outperformed them all.

General Observations on the Four Companies

Emerson Electric had an enormous total market value; it was compared with Zenith Radio, which did not fare well, and Graham observed, "High valuations entail high risks."

Emery Air Freight was considered the most promising of the four; although it was pointed out that it is easier to multiply a small capitalization than a large, Emery had done well even in bad market years.

Emhart did better in its business than the market pricing suggested and it had not outperformed the DJIA.

ELTRA was the same—good performance not reflected on the market.

Conclusions: Analysts will find Emhart and ELTRA the most appealing of the four because of better market action and faster recent growth in earnings. Of these two factors, Graham considered the first invalid for consideration by conservative investors, and the second had only limited validity. Although Emery appeared to be a successful business, the high P/E ratio of 60 makes the decision to buy such an expensive pick extremely risky. For growth investors, it might make for a valid buy— but, again, not for the conservative investor. (Note: the P/E ratio later fell to 15 with poor earnings.) Emerson Electric appeared overvalued, the market giving it the benefit of a billion dollars against future earnings. ELTRA and Emhart were both priced low, virtually at book value. The rate of earnings on invested capital and the stability of profits were both satisfactory. As such they met Graham's seven criteria for inclusion in a defensive portfolio:

1. Adequate size
2. Strong financial condition
3. Continued dividends for at least the previous twenty years
4. No earnings deficit in the previous ten years
5. Ten-year growth of at least one-third in per-share earnings
6. Price of stock no more than 1.5 times net asset value
7. Price no more than fifteen times average earnings in previous three years.

Although Graham preferred Emhart and ELTRA for new purchase, he did not think an analyst would have suggested getting out of Emerson or Emery in exchange for their shares since both of those companies were performing satisfactorily.

CHAPTER 14
STOCK SELECTION
FOR THE DEFENSIVE INVESTOR

CHAPTER SUMMARY

In this chapter, seven quantitative criteria/guidelines are examined for the defensive investor. For the whole portfolio, the earnings-to-price ratio (E/P) should be at least as high as the current high-grade bond rate. By applying quantitative criteria, Graham shows how the thirty DIJA stocks in 1970 are filtered down to just five. It is argued that the defensive investor should sell stocks that have exceeded their value and potential. Although capital gains tax must be paid, this approach is better than not selling the stock and thus having it retract in value. It is further argued that there are only a few rules that the defensive investor must apply to be successful with his stock selection strategy.

CHAPTER OUTLINE

The defensive investor will select only high-grade bonds and choose from a diversified list of leading common stocks whose price is not unduly high. The list may either be based on the Dow Jones Industrial Average (DJIA) or on quantitative testing.

If chosen from the DJIA, the selection could include small samples from each of the leading issues and the growth companies, or, with less effort, the investor could buy into an investment fund that is indexed to the Dow.

If chosen through quantitative criteria, the investor should ensure a minimum of *quality* in past performance and current financial position, and a minimum of *quantity* in terms of assets and earnings per dollar (Note: this would most likely be ROE, but it's not specifically mentioned by name).

1. *Adequate Size of the Enterprise:* Exclude small companies; some may have possibilities, but the group as a whole is not suited to the defensive investor.

2. *Sufficiently Strong Financial Condition:* Current assets should be at least double current liabilities, known as the "Two-to-One ratio." This means the current ratio should be higher than 2.0. Long-term debt should not exceed working capital. For public utilities, debt should not be greater than double the book value of stock equity. This means the debt/equity should remain under 2.0.

3. *Earnings Stability:* At least some earnings declared in all preceding ten years.

4. *Dividend Record:* Uninterrupted payments for at least twenty years.

5. *Earnings Growth:* Minimum increase of at least a third in per-share earnings in previous ten years, using three-year averages at beginning and end.

6. *Moderate Price/Earnings Ratio:* Current price should not exceed 15 times earnings averaged over previous three years.

7. *Moderate Ratio of Price to Assets:* Current price should not exceed 150% of last reported book value, with allowance for a lower P/E but selling at higher proportion to book value (e.g. P/E of 9, at 250% book value would be acceptable).

General Comments: the above seven requirements are addressed to the defensive investor, who must exclude companies that: a) are too small; b) are in weak financial state; c) have deficit stigma during the previous ten years; d) have insufficient history of dividend payments. Of these deficiencies, weak financial strength is the most concerning.

Many analysts recommend paying premium prices to purchase choice companies. Graham plainly states that he holds the contrary view, for such stocks lack an essential *margin of safety* against a downturn in the market.

The suggested P/E ratio of 15 is a *maximum*, and the portfolio might well average several points less than that; the average (reversed) earnings-to-price ratio (E/P) for the whole portfolio should be at least as high as the current high-grade bond rate.

Application of Our Criteria to the DJIA at the End of 1970

In this section of the book, Graham lists thirty stocks that each meets at least one of the seven criteria found in the first section. After listing the thirty stocks and their corresponding metrics, Graham mentions that only five of the picks meet all seven criteria on their own. The example is to illustrate how his criteria help filter results.

- Note: With the advent of Google stock screeners, the investor can quickly apply his criteria with little to no effort when finding potential picks.

The Public Utility "Solution"

There is a Dow Jones list of public utilities. Fifteen of these in 1972 met Graham's listed criteria for suitability to include in the conservative investor's portfolio, and their dividend return was significantly higher than the average common stocks on the DJIA. He considered their position as effective monopolies, with the right to adjust charges to meet the need for capital expansion, to be an advantage to the investor. P/E ratios are modest; rise in profit has not matched industrial issues but the utilities have shown stability of price at times when the industrial issues did not.

Even the defensive investor should be willing to change items in his portfolio when they appear to have advanced to their potential limit and advantages could be found in other stocks. Capital gains might have to be paid, but experience has shown, "It is better to sell and pay the tax than not sell and repent."

Investing in Stocks of Financial Enterprises

The field comprises banks, commercial banks, insurance companies, savings and loan associations (S&L), mortgage companies, investment companies with their mutual funds, consumer finance companies with their credit cards, real estate investment trusts, and numerous others. It is characterized by small proportions of assets in material objects and a high proportion of short-term debt in excess of stock capital. Financial soundness becomes the issue, and in consequence there are extensive regulations and supervisory mechanisms.

Shares in financial concerns have produced results equivalent to other common stocks. Graham seems to be lukewarm about them and recommends applying the same arithmetical standards for price-to-earnings and book value that the conservative investor would apply to other companies.

Railroad Issues

The railroads have suffered severely from both competition and regulation, not to mention the rising cost of labor. In the last half-century, half the railroad mileage has been bankrupt. The unanticipated failures of some railroads, notably the Penn Central, has made analysts wary of recommending the group. It did well during the war, and some have done better than others. Graham feels it is as unfair and unreasonable to condemn an entire industry as it is to recommend one, but points out that, "There is no compelling reason to own railroad stock."

Selectivity for the Defensive Investor

Every investor thinks the performance of his portfolio should exceed the average, and that is why he engages the services of an adviser.

It is suggested that if 100 security analysts were asked to pick their "five best," there would be a wide difference in their choices. But the explanation for this is based on the belief that the market is efficient in pricing stocks according to the known relevant data (the efficient markets hypothesis or EMH), and one pick is therefore as good as another. If all analysts were in agreement, the price of the stock would change according to their opinions.

The reputation of the security analyst is founded not on his research of what *has* happened (no great skill needed) but on forecasting what *will* happen (great skill needed). To this end he may practice either *prediction* or *protection,* recognizing that investments are made in the *present* but are about the *future,* which remains entirely uncertain.

Prediction requires an estimate of the company's behavior in future years. This becomes dangerous when forecasting unsustainable growth into the future, or, by more sophisticated analysis of supply and demand for the company's product or services, and a measure of volume, price and costs. This is the *qualitative approach,* which emphasizes non-measurable estimates of prospects and management. Some analysts, persuaded by their belief in future profits, might recommend a stock without regard to its current market price (clearly Graham was not one of them).

Protection requires attention to the price of the stock, and as such is sought when indicated present value is above market price, leaving the required margin of safety. The analyst's enthusiasm for a particular stock will rest less on its future profits than on its future stability. This is the *quantitative (statistical) approach,* which emphasizes measurable relationships.

Graham states he was always of the quantitative persuasion, to ensure value for money, and not interested in uncertain promises of profit that did not fit the figures. He concedes that other analysts do not all subscribe to his views, and that probably the majority favor an intangible "human factor" over cold figures seen on the balance sheet.

The advice given: The defensive investor should emphasize diversification within the four rules of selection already described.

CHAPTER 15
STOCK SELECTION
FOR THE ENTERPRISING INVESTOR

CHAPTER SUMMARY

This chapter discusses why it is difficult for the enterprising investor to perform better than the market average, which large mutual funds and analysts as a whole have failed to do. One option is the efficient market hypothesis, while another is the favoring of popular stocks. The enterprising investor may benefit from sound unpopular securities, and Benjamin Graham gives a brief review of five methods he has been applying himself.

The enterprising investor can benefit from a combination of various quantitative criteria before studying the stock further. Looking at only one criterion may lead to less-than-stellar performance. Finally, the chapter looks at bargains that can be made in special circumstances; for instance, when the stock is priced below net working capital.

CHAPTER OUTLINE

The emphasis on advice for the conservative investor was principally on exclusions—what not to buy—advising against purchase of both poor-quality and overly high-priced issues. For the enterprising investor, the advice will be based on the selection of individual issues seen as likely to have a better-than-average future performance. But Graham states that he doubts the ability to do this.

Average results are easily obtained—buy the index. To the uniformed, the idea of outperforming the average through the application of skill and knowledge may seem easy; however, the evidence accumulated from those who have set out to do this does not support this notion.

The large mutual funds, sufficiently financed to pay for the best advice, have failed over the years to keep up with the S&P 500 index, and research studies have shown that random selection of stock performed as well or better than the highly paid choices of the experts. In general, the margin of underperformance corresponded closely to the cost of operating the fund. However, the funds are valuable in that they make the market available to the small investor who, left to make his own choices, will in general underperform the market to a substantially greater extent than will the funds.

There are two explanations given for the failure to outperform the market. The first is the efficient market theory that, at the time it is offered, the price of the stock is appropriate in light of all that is known about it. As such, future severe out-of-the-ordinary changes were therefore not predictable—and the analyst cannot be expected to predict the unpredictable. There are literally thousands of experts at work; they freely share their opinions and, reasonably, the consensus is the going price.

The second possibility offered to explain analysts' failure to outperform the market is their chosen method of favoring the companies with a good record of performance and sound management, assuming it will continue to succeed in the future because it did in the past. As such, if the analyst discriminates against a large section of the market that does not have such a history, perhaps the enterprising investor may find what he seeks in that segment. The problem of analysts is too *much* skill, not too *little*, so between the thousands of them at work, they are likely to have set an inappropriate price—resulting in their failure as a whole.

A Summary of the Graham-Newman Method

The corporation operated from 1926 to 1956; the following is the classification of the sophisticated instruments employed.

Arbitrages: Simultaneous purchase of a security and the sale of other securities for which it was to be exchanged.

Liquidations: Purchase of shares for which cash payments were to be made on liquidation of a company's assets.

Arbitrages and Liquidations were selected when there was a calculated rate of return of 20% and an 80% chance of success.

Related Hedges: Simultaneous purchase of convertible bonds (or convertible preferred shares) and sale of equivalent common stock for which they were exchangeable; profit comes when the common stock price falls below the convertible issue.

Net-Current-Asset ("Bargain") Issues: Purchase of at least 100 different issues when cost was less than two-thirds book value.

During the time the corporation operated, it was found that apparently attractive issues obtainable at less than their working capital based on analysis did not pan out, and they subsequently abandoned the approach. They also abandoned the hedging of unrelated hedging operations. So from 1939 onwards, there were only self-liquidating situations, related hedging, and working capital bargains in the portfolio. Beyond stating, "Each of these classes gave us quite consistently satisfactory results," Graham does not detail the amount of his successes.

The choice of instruments in this corporation might be narrower than what other aggressive investors might select; they might enter a field where the securities were not overvalued by conservative measures and which past records or other features have made attractive. They should nevertheless apply all the measures of analysis suggested—but perhaps allowing, for example, an unusually high rating in one factor to outweigh or balance a less-than-desirable rating on another. Choices should be confined to an industry about which the investor feels optimistic, but enthusiasm will not justify paying too high a price for a stock. The purchase of cyclical stocks (e.g., steel) at the bottom swing in the market is suggested. Yesterday's losers are often tomorrow's winners.

Secondary Companies

For possible selection by the enterprising investor are those companies that have been successful but are not in popular favor, such as ELTRA and Emhart, which were already described.

There are various ways of finding such companies. Here, Graham refers to the Standard & Poor's *Stock Guide*, published monthly for sale but also supplied gratuitously by some brokers to their clients. In the 230 pages of the guide, condensed information is given on all companies listed on the exchanges and unlisted companies (4,500 at the time of writing). Graham describes the pages as presenting, "A condensed panorama of the splendors and miseries of the stock market... all kinds of Wall Street gadgets and widgets, they are all there, waiting to be browsed over, or studied with a serious objective."

A Winnowing of the Stock Guide

Suggested: search for low price related to earnings as given in the guide, and list those with a ratio of nine or less. Twenty meeting this requirement were selected in alphabetic order, all starting with an "A." To these twenty stocks should be applied the same analytic criteria as outlined for the defensive investor:

1. *Financial Condition:* Current assets at least 150% of current liabilities; debt not more than 110% of net current assets.
2. *Earnings Stability:* No deficit in the preceding five years.
3. *Dividend Record:* Some current dividend.
4. *Earnings Growth:* Previous year's earnings more than four years before.
5. *Price:* Less than 120% of net tangible assets.

These criteria applied to the random group of twenty stocks reduced it to five that met the requirements, and it was suggested that the investor should continue the exercise until he had found 15 that did— there are possibly 150 in the guide that would. S&P offer a ranking, and if the investor followed that (another criterion to employ) the number of acceptable stocks would be reduced to 100. From these, the enterprising investor could follow his whims and select 20% of them.

Single Criteria for Choosing Common Stocks

Would it be possible to simplify the work and use only one of these several criteria? The individual criteria associated with satisfactory selections have been low-multiplier stocks of important companies, and a diversified group selling below working capital (net current asset) value. The former, in practice, did not do as well, and the latter is too hard to find to be of practical value.

The S&P guide conveniently has columns of figures that allow an analysis to be made against certain criteria selected:

1. Low P/E
2. High dividend return
3. Very long dividend record
4. Very large enterprise measured by number of outstanding shares
5. Strong financial position
6. Low price per share
7. Low price in relation to previous high price
8. High S&P ranking.

Stocks were randomly chosen, based on the individual criteria, and comprised three portfolios of thirty stocks. During the time period under examination, the DJIA declined 5%, but the portfolios declined an average of 22%. The moral to be drawn: avoid second-quality issues (or common stocks) unless they are hard-core bargains across many different criteria.

Other findings in this retrospective analytic experiment:

1. Three groups outperformed the DJIA—they were industrials with an A+ rating, outdoing the Dow by 17%; whereas utilities with an A+ rating declined markedly.
2. Large companies showed no change during the time the Dow declined slightly.
3. Stocks sold at a high price, over $100, showed a 1% advance.

The "goodwill component:" This is the margin by which price exceeds book value. It was found (contrary to established investment philosophy) that major companies with a large goodwill component in their market price did very well. "Goodwill giants" were the best performers, and the explanations offered were: momentum; excellent earnings record; public expectation of continued excellent performance; strong market action. Although their performance might seem to recommend these "goodwill giants" for a diversified portfolio, Graham's preference was for the criteria previously described.

- Note: Warren Buffett disagrees with this recommendation. He gains a margin of safety with "Goodwill Giants" by investing in companies with a durable competitive advantage—like Coke.

Other tests using a single criterion with favorable results did not change his opinion that multiple criteria should be applied.

Bargain Issues, or Net-Current-Asset Stocks

The S&P Stock Guide made available a number of companies whose stocks were trading at a price below their working capital, defined for this purpose as per-share value of current assets minus liabilities. Fifty could be found; the ones that had performed poorly had net losses and were rejected from the study group, but this left a number of companies with well-known brand names that had for incomprehensible reasons done the reverse of "goodwill" and fallen out of the public's favor. Yes, money can be made on bargain issues if you can find them, and if you are patient once you have bought them.

Another anomaly is the ability of shares of a new and untried company launched into a bull market to outstrip those of the tried and true majors; their ultimate collapse in price is inevitable.

Special Situations or "Workouts"

Situation #1: Borden (at 26) announced their intention to buy Kayser-Roth (at 28) by exchanging 1.5 of their shares for 1 of the others, respectively. If the purchase had been made of 300 Kayser-Roth and sales of 400 Borden, the return on investment in six months would have been at a 40% per annum rate.

Situation #2: National Biscuit offered to buy Aurora Plastics at $11 per share when it was selling at $8.5; it sold at 9 through the following month.

Situation #3: Universal-Marion had ceased business and went into liquidation; the common stock had a book value of $28.5; the stock closed at $21.5 leaving room for a 30% profit.

Special situations are a special business. Many billions are spent in mergers and acquisitions, and "special situations" are found, but it needs an alert, capable person to profit from them. Many announced mergers never happen and buying against the possibility of profit might result in the probability of a loss. In fact, a review of the above situations conducted at a later date showed them not to be nearly as profitable as it first appeared.

Conclusion: Merger arbitrage is wholly inappropriate for most individual investors.

CHAPTER 16
CONVERTIBLE ISSUES AND WARRANTS

CHAPTER SUMMARY

This chapter examines convertibility. By its very nature, convertibility is neither attractive nor unattractive, as it all depends on the facts surrounding the buy. General guidelines are provided for the investor who considers engaging in convertible securities, and special cases are considered; for example, Graham strongly discourages the defensive investor from buying into companies which have large amounts of stock option warrants outstanding. More examples are provided throughout the chapter.

CHAPTER OUTLINE

More than half of the preferred issues in the S&P Stock Guide have conversion privileges (this means preferred shares can be turned into common stock); there are convertible bonds and stock-option warrants giving the right to buy shares at a stipulated price, which were listed by the NYSE for the first time in 1970.

- Note: the next section refers to warrants. A warrant is an agreement between a holder and an issuer on the value of an underlying asset. The agreement specifies the holder's rights to purchase equity of the business at a specific price and within a certain timeframe. This is very similar to an option. The difference is that warrants are issued and guaranteed by the company and options are not.

Convertible issues (at the time of writing) are much more important than warrants; they will be considered from the points of view of their value as an investment opportunity and their effect on the value of common shares. From the investor's viewpoint he has the superior protection of a bond as well as an opportunity to enter the market should the price of the common stock make it advantageous—seemingly a "win-win" situation.

But does life really have "win-win" situations? What Wall Street gives with one hand it usually takes away with the other. The investor must be giving up something either in quality or yield for the privilege of conversion; if the company gets its money at lower cost, it surrenders part of the shareholder's claim to future enhancement.

Convertible issues are neither attractive nor unattractive—it all depends on the ascertainable facts. Experience has shown that convertible issues floated at the peak of a bull market may appear favorable, but when looked at closer, prove unsatisfactory.

Convertible securities are not necessarily less attractive than non-convertible securities. There is more security in the convertible bond than in the stock, but the chances are the stock was overpriced when the bond was issued. The investor also has to face the question of timing: when it has become attractive to turn in the bond because the share price has now appreciated, should he do that or should he wait for a further appreciation in value?

During a bull market, convertible bonds did well because share prices rose, but clearly they do less well in a declining market. There is a Wall Street maxim, "Never convert a convertible bond." The teaching is to sell the bond when its value has appreciated, not to hold the shares which might decline and then all profit is lost.

Look more than twice before buying convertible issues; the ideal is a strongly secured convertible, exchangeable for an attractive common stock at a price only slightly higher than the current market rate. Such an opportunity is more likely to be found with older rather than new issues.

Effect of Convertible Issues on the Status of the Common Stock

There is a tendency to offer convertible issues when mergers and acquisitions occur, which may result in reported increase in earnings per share, but also has the potential for dilution of share value should the conversions occur. This is something investors need to be cognizant of as they consider such a security.

Indicated Switches from Common into Preferred Stocks

Before 1956, common stock almost always yielded better results than preferred stock. At the time Graham was writing this book, he suggested the opposite was true. He states that the market may offer preferred stock, which is more attractive to hold than the common stock of the company, and the investor may find an advantage in switching from junior to senior issues. Graham then provides an example with the Studebaker-Worthington Corp. In the example, the investor could get a better return and more security with an exchange from common stock to preferred stock.

Stock-Option Warrants

"We consider the recent development of stock-option warrants as a near fraud."

"They have created huge aggregate dollar 'values' out of thin air."

"They have no excuse for existence."

"They should be prohibited by law."

These quotations can leave no doubt of Graham's views on warrants. In the usual company report, the earnings per share are usually calculated without consideration of the exercise of outstanding warrants.

The shareholder who has first rights to buy new shares is displaced by the warrant holder. The company that issues the warrants has no way of requiring them to be exercised when the company needs to expand its capital; the holder may or may not buy the shares, as he wishes.

It's safe to say that Graham would most likely discourage defensive investors from even considering such a pick, which has large amounts of warrants outstanding.

Practical Postscript

Nearly all new warrants are valid for a fixed number of years. Some older warrants were open in perpetuity (or, in other words, forever). "The main objective of our attack on warrants as a financial mechanism is... to argue against the wanton creation of huge 'paper-money' monstrosities."

In this quote, Graham essentially says that warrants are nothing more than gambles that involve large sums of money and are outrageously wrong for investors and businesses alike.

CHAPTER 17
FOUR EXTREMELY
INSTRUCTIVE CASE HISTORIES

CHAPTER SUMMARY

Four companies are reviewed to instruct investors in the detection of severe warning signs. For Penn Central Co., fundamental weaknesses were revealed, ranging from no income tax paid for eleven years, to strange transactions that were too odd and complex to describe. Ling-Temco-Vought Inc., which grew twentyfold in just two years, fueled its expansion through too much debt willingly supplied by commercial banks. NFV Corp acquired a much larger company using warrants and debts sold at odd prices, while having almost no equity on the balance sheet. This was a case study in bad management, which ultimately led to a conviction. AAA Enterprises traded at unreasonable prices compared to earnings and equity, showing conscious and unconscious investor speculation before the company went bankrupt.

CHAPTER OUTLINE

The histories in question represent "extremes" on Wall Street, and are instructive warnings for investors at every stage of competence and experience.

Penn Central (Railroad) Co: An extreme example of the neglect of the most elementary warning signals, resulting in a crazily high market price for a tottering giant.

Ling-Temco-Vought Inc.: An extreme example of quick and unsound "empire-building" with collapse helped by indiscriminate bank lending.

NVF Corp: An extreme example of corporate acquisition, with a small company absorbing another seven times its size, incurring huge debt and employing startling accounting devices.

AAA Enterprises: An extreme example of public-stock financing of a small company using the magic word "franchising."

The Penn Central Case

In terms of assets and revenues, this was the country's largest railroad. In 1970 it went bankrupt and defaulted on its bond issues, shocking the financial world. The share price fell from 86½ to 5½. The simplest application of the rules of security analysis would have revealed the fundamental weakness long before bankruptcy occurred.

1. Graham regards the minimum coverage for railroad bonds to be five times earnings before taxes or 2,9 times earnings after taxes; the Penn Central was operating at 1.98. They had paid no income tax for 11 years; hence the coverage was less than two times, totally failing to meet the required five.

2. Considering the company paid no income tax for numerous years, red flags should have been raised into the validity of their reported earnings.

3. The bonds could have been exchanged in the years before collapse for better secured issues.

4. Earnings of $3.80 per share were reported in 1968, when the market price was 86½; that is, a P/E of 24. Clearly the reality of the earnings in the absence of tax payments should have been questioned.

5. There was a merger in 1966, when earnings of $6.80 were reported. A few years later, a special charge was incurred on the "cost and losses" account for $12 a share. Only in a "fairyland called Wall Street" can a company claim $6.80 in earnings only to turn around and claim a $12 loss.

6. The transportation ratio is the expense of running the train divided by total revenues: the higher the ratio, the less efficient the railroad. An analyst should have spotted that the Penn Central transportation ratio was 47.5%, whereas the comparable Norfolk and Western was 35.2%.

7. Strange transactions with peculiar accounting were found, but details are too complex to describe.

Conclusion: it is not clear that the railroad could have been saved, but analysts ought to have spotted what was coming and financial corrective measures should have been taken. Graham draws a moral: "Security analysts should do their elementary jobs before they study stock market movements, gaze into crystal balls, make elaborate mathematical calculations..." A simple look at the P/E ratio would have identified this company as undesirable.

Ling-Temco-Vought Inc.

Head-over-heels expansion into head-over-heels debt

Founded by the iconic "young genius," this was a small company that grew twentyfold in two years, then continued to grow exponentially from initial sales of $7 million to reported sales of $2.8 billion and a debt of 1.7 billion. Then the stock price fell from 169½ to 24 and the founding genius was moved aside—but too late. Stock price fell nearly to $7, and the bond issue was quoted at 15 cents on the dollar.

The company had entered into "serial acquisition," buying up one company after another; serial acquisition is likened to serial killing since it usually results in deaths of all companies concerned. They practiced "kitchen-sink" accounting, putting all possible reserves and bad debts into one year so the other years would shine. The extraordinary (or is it?) thing about it was the fact that the banks with their financial analysts were financing LTV to the tune of supporting long-term debt of 1.869 billion. The company's coverage of interest charges did not meet conservative standards, despite the fact that the banks provided $400 million for further "diversification." (In later years, the banks were to do the same with Enron and WorldCom, among numerous other financial disasters.)

The NVF Takeover of Sharon Steel (A Collector's Item)

The business was described as "vulcanized fiber and plastics," and had an income of $502,000. They decided they would take over Sharon Steel, which was seven times larger than NVF and had net earnings of nearly three million dollars. The management of Sharon Steel vainly resisted the takeover funded by warrants on NTV and bonds that sold at 42 cents on the dollar—surely a warning sign.

After the takeover, the company's report showed "deferred debt expense" of $58,600,000 listed as an asset, but greater than the stockholders' equity of $40,200,000; not included in the shareholders' equity was $20,700,000 labeled, "Excess of equity over cost of investment in Sharon."

There followed a series of accounting maneuvers that no analyst could be expected to understand, but that appeared to be directed at obtaining a tax advantage. At the end of 1970, the S&P Guide showed the P/E ratio for NTV was two, the lowest figure in their guide comprising 4,500 issues—which corroborates the argument that if it sounds too good to be true, it probably is.

In 1972, court decisions regarding NTV found that the chairman, Victor Posner, had improperly diverted pension assets of Sharon Steel to assist affiliated companies in their takeovers of other corporations. In 1977, the SEC obtained an injunction against Posner to prevent him from future violations of Federal laws against securities fraud. It was alleged that he had improperly obtained from NTV and Sharon $1.7 million in personal perks, had overstated Sharon's pre-tax earnings by $13.9 million, and had shifted income and expenses from one year to another. Sharon Steel became known in Wall Street as "Share and Steal."

- Note: In later years, Victor Posner became a major player in the junk bonds underwritten by Drexel Burnham Lambert. In 1988, the SEC sued Drexel Burnham Lambert and charged Victor Posner with scheming to conceal Posner's purchase of stock in the electrical contractor, Fischbach Corporation. A bankruptcy judge ordered him to return several original paintings to the Sharon Steel Corporation, which he had removed from the company's headquarters when he acquired the company. In 1988, three million dollars in charitable donations were ordered as part of a sentence for tax evasion. He was also required to work 5000 hours of community service time. In 1993, both he and his son, Steven Posner, were barred by the SEC from being an officer or director of a public company.

AAA Enterprises

In 1958, Jackie Williams founded a company to sell mobile homes (then called trailers). The stock rose 56% on the day it was issued. He incorporated the business in 1965, and that year made pre-tax $61,000 on $5,800,000 sales. In 1968, he franchised his business. He started "Mr

Tax of America," a company doing tax returns while housed in one of the trailers, and he franchised that. Shares were sold on his company, which appeared first in the S&P Guide (due to the AAA) and were at a price of 115 times earnings. From the launching of shares, Williams received $3,600,000 and the companies that handled it received $500,000.

Those who purchased the shares, which had an earnings value of seven cents each, were (consciously or unconsciously) speculating heavily on the potential of future profit; however, the price of the shares doubled. AAA expanded its business empire by opening a chain of carpet stores and buying the plant that made the mobile homes; it went on to report a loss of $1.49 per share ($4,365,000), which reduced its capital to eight cents for each of the shares that had been purchased for $13.

Ultimately, the company went into receivership in 1971 despite Williams's attempt to prevent this with $2,500,000 of his own money.

Moral and (rhetorical) Questions

Graham entered Wall Street in 1914 and expressed his opinion that ethical standards had fallen (even further) in the fifty-seven years of his experience. He recognized that the "Speculative public is incorrigible... it will buy anything at any price if there seems to be some action in progress," which led him to pose these questions:

Should not responsible investment houses be honor-bound to refrain from identifying themselves with such enterprises, nine out of ten of which are doomed to failure?

Could and should the SEC be given other powers to protect the public?

Should some kind of box-score for public offerings of various types be compiled and published in a conspicuous fashion?

Should every prospectus... carry some kind of formal warranty that the offering price for the issue is not substantially out of line with the ruling prices... already established in the market?

CHAPTER 18
A COMPARISON OF
EIGHT PAIRS OF COMPANIES

CHAPTER SUMMARY

In this chapter, companies are examined in eight seemingly similar pairs, and the reason for their change in circumstances is explained. The takeaway from the comparison includes the importance of buying securities priced at low and reasonable multiples compared to both net assets and earnings. Also, the importance of turning revenue into profit is discussed, and warnings provided about buying into too much goodwill.

CHAPTER OUTLINE

By taking two companies that appear close to each other, Graham intends to expose the varieties of character in their financial structure, policies, and performance.

Pair 1. Real Estate Investment Trust (stores, offices, factories, etc.) and Realty Equities Corp. of New York (real estate investment, general construction)

Of these two companies—both listed on the American Stock Exchange, with similar ticker symbols (REI & REC)—one is a staid New England trust with a history dating to 1889, and the other is a New York sudden-growth venture.

In 1960, both corporations had a stable profile; the Investment Trust had .66 earnings per share and Realty Equities .47. Eight years later, the Investment Trust was in much the same state, but the Realty Equities, "Had metamorphosed into something monstrous and vulnerable," having moved out of pure real estate holdings into the purchase of two race tracks, seventy-four movie theaters, three literary agencies, a public relations firm, hotels, supermarkets and a cosmetics firm.

Graham's interest is in the reaction of the market. The tried-and-true Trust was virtually ignored despite the increase in share value from twenty to thirty. On the other hand, Realty Equities received much attention; stock went from ten to thirty-seven, warrants went from six to thirty-six, even though their asset value as judged by the balance sheet was only $3.41 per share, while by contrast the book value of the Trust shares was $20.85.

A year later, the price of the Realty Equities shares fell to 9½, though the directors continued to pay a dividend of five cents per share. The auditors refused to certify the statements, the company was delisted by the ASE and the share price fell to $2. The shares of the Trust continued to keep their value.

Pair 2. Air Products and Chemicals (industrial and medical gases etc.) and Air Reduction Co. (industrial gases and equipment; chemicals)

These companies resemble each other both in their name and in their type of business. Air Products was a newer company than Air Reduction and in consequence had less than half their volume of sales; however, it showed a stronger growth and greater profitability and sold at a P/E of nine compared with a P/E of 16½ for its competitor. Air Reduction paid a higher dividend and had more working capital.

The issue discussed: how in relative terms would an analyst view these two companies? The figures suggest Air Products has more promise, but was it a better buy considering its higher price? The Street sets "quality" above "quantity," which suggested that analysts would prefer the apparently better corporation, Air Products, despite the higher price of the shares. Air Reduction, however, was in the class of "important companies with low multiples," which was favorable.

As the years passed and the market declined, Air Products stood up better; however, Air Reduction made a later comeback, gaining 50% over its low in comparison with the 30% gained by Air Products.

Pair 3. American Home Products Co. (drugs, cosmetics, household products, candy) and American Hospital Supply Co. (distributor and manufacturer of hospital supplies and equipment)

Two rapidly growing and immensely profitable companies both showing strong financial conditions. Although the growth rate of "Hospital" exceeded that of "Home," the latter had better profitability. P/E ratios for Hospital and Home were respectively 58.5 and 31.0.

Graham concludes that both companies are "Too rich" to be recommended for conservative investment, that their price was based more on promise than on performance, and that there was far too much "goodwill" in it. In later years, Hospital (acquired by Baxter Healthcare) sold at a loss of 30% whereas Home (later Wyeth) retained its price.

Pair 4. H&R Block Inc. (income tax service) and Blue Bell, Inc. (manufacturers of work clothes, uniforms, etc.)

Blue Bell was a long established company (1916) with unbroken dividend history from 1923. Block's first figures were for 1961; it had a meteoric rise and gained a P/E of 108 compared with Bell at eleven. Respective prices per share were 55 and 49. Blue Bell was doing four times as much business and gave nine times the dividend yield on price.

Graham feels an experienced analyst would have been impressed with Block but might think the company was already fully valued or even overvalued; in contrast, Blue Bell would have been easy to recommend for its conservative price. When the market turned down, both companies lost, then both recovered, Blue Bell better than Block. Clearly Blue Bell was a better buy, but Block would not have been a bad choice, proving that an apparently overvalued stock can stay the course and remain overvalued—a discouragement to short sellers.

Pair 5. International Flavors & Fragrances (flavors, etc., for other businesses) and International Harvester Co. (truck manufacturer, farm machinery, construction machinery)

These are adjacent corporations on the NYSE list. International Harvester is certainly the better known, but "Flavors" was selling at a higher market value than "Harvester," explained on the grounds of profitability and growth. Flavors showed a profit of 14.3% on sales compared with 2.6% for Harvester; Flavors had a return of 19.7% on capital compared with Harvester's 5.5%. Over a period of five years, Flavors' sales doubled, Harvester's remained virtually unchanged. Flavors sold at a P/E of 55, Harvester at 10.7.

Flavor's success was completely straightforward—no accounting gimmicks, just success in sales. By contrast, Harvester had sales of $2½ billion dollars but an unimpressive profit. Graham asks, "What is the point in doing so much business if the shareholder receives so little on his investment?"

From the point of view of conservative investment, Flavors would not have been acceptable because it was "lavishly valued," and Harvester, although low-priced, would not have been acceptable because of its underperformance. When the market downturn occurred, Flavors was hit harder than Harvester, losing 30%, but then recovered and continued its rise in price, which Harvester did not.

Pair 6. McGraw Edison (public utility and equipment; housewares) and McGraw-Hill, Inc. (books, films, instruction systems; magazine and newspaper publishers; information services)

Called here "Edison" and "Hill" for convenience, these were totally different companies selling at about the same price but because of Hill's larger capitalization it was valued at twice the figure for Edison, despite Edison having 50% higher sales and 25% better net earnings. This gave a P/E to Hill twice that of Edison (35 versus 15.5).

The price of Hill shares represented a goodwill component of more than a billion dollars, an example of "The triumph of hope over experience."

During the following two years, Hill's shares declined to 20% of previous value, then recovered to 60%, whereas Edison recovered fully. Although McGraw-Hill remained a strong and prosperous company, its price history exemplified its speculative character.

Pair 7. National General Corp. (a large conglomerate) and National Presto Industries (diversified electric appliances, ordnance)

Designated "General" and "Presto" for convenience.

Presto's capital structure was simplicity itself: 1½ million shares of common stock selling at $58 million dollars.

General had more than twice as many shares, an issue of convertible preferred, three issues of stock warrants, towering convertible bond issue and a "goodly sum" of non-convertible bonds. Market capitalization of $534 million with other issues pending amounting to $750 million.

Despite General's higher capitalization, the corporation had only 75% of Presto's net income.

Graham discusses the significance of General's warrants and the effect on dilution, as well as the manner in which the accounts were reported. He believes them to be part of the "common stock package" that raises the true market price of the common stock to be twice that quoted, which computes to an "inherently absurd" P/E of 69 (compared with Presto at 6.9).

Presto met all the requirements of a sound and reasonably priced investment. General "Had all the earmarks of a typical conglomerate of late 1960s vintage, full of corporate gadgets and grandiose gestures, but lacking in substantial values behind the market quotations."

Pair 8. Whiting Corp. (materials-handling equipment) and Willcox & Gibbs (small conglomerate)

The market share price for these two companies was about equal, with Willcox at 15.5 and Whiting at 17.75, which in Graham's terms, "Makes one wonder if Wall Street is a rational institution."

Willcox had smaller sales and earnings, half the tangible assets for the common, was about to report a large loss, and had not paid a dividend in thirteen years. The company was founded in 1866 when they made industrial sewing machines; subsequently they expanded to absorb twenty-four subsidiary companies making a wide variety of products, but were, in Wall Street terms, a small conglomerate. P/E ratio was "very large."

Whiting had a record of satisfactory earnings, paid dividends regularly since 1936, and had one of the highest dividend yields in the list. The company was founded in 1896 and continued, as it started, in the materials-handling field. P/E ratio was 9.3.

CHAPTER 19
SHAREHOLDERS AND MANAGEMENTS: DIVIDEND POLICY

CHAPTER SUMMARY

This chapter argues that shareholders prefer a more liberal payout policy, while management prefers to retain the earnings inside the company. As shareholders can argue that profit belongs to them, the counter-argument is that it can be employed for growth, ultimately benefitting the shareholder. Benjamin Graham argues that dividends should either be paid out or shareholders should demand the profitability of retaining earnings to be proven. The tax advantage of stock dividends compared to cash dividends is also highlighted, followed by a strong opinion about written dividend policies.

CHAPTER OUTLINE

Shareholders are justified in asking questions as to the competence of the management when the results:

1. "Are unsatisfactory in themselves."
2. "Are poorer than those obtained by other companies that appear similarly situated."
3. "Have resulted in an unsatisfactory market price of long duration."

With very few exceptions, poor management has changed as a result of the "public stockholders." Instead, control is usually impacted by an individual or compact group. As a consequence, boards of directors are more active these days in terms of their fundamental duty to see that their company has sound management.

The change has often occurred after many long years of bad results without remedial action. Individual shareholders have found making their presence felt at annual meetings was generally a futile performance.

Shareholders and Dividend Policy

In general, shareholders want liberal dividends while management wants to "Keep the money in the business to strengthen the business." The basic argument for paying small dividends is not that the company needs the money, but that it can be used to the shareholders' direct benefit by using the funds for profitable expansion. The current practice is retention of a large part of the profits instead of the older practice of paying 75% of profit in dividends. Note: At the end of the nineties, the payout ratio was between 35% and 40%. Payout ratio is the dividend rate divided by the EPS.

The argument for paying out rather than retaining profit is that the profits "belong" to the shareholders and many might need the capital to support their lifestyle. This used to have an effect on the market, which tended to favor the companies with a liberal dividend policy. It is now more common, however, particularly with new technology issues, to find a "profitable reinvestment" policy where investors accept small or no dividends as long as the company shows growth. Where prime emphasis is not placed on growth, the stock is rated as an "income issue" and the dividend is the primary means for determining the market price. When the stock is clearly classified as "growth," the dividend is of lesser importance. Many companies are in an intermediate role, and, even though the company may lack growth, it may still pay no dividend, so it can retain capital and later employ it for future growth.

Graham expresses the view that shareholders should demand one or the other—disburse two-thirds of the profits as dividends or show evidence of their use for growth as measured by per-share earnings. There is no reason to believe owners will benefit from expansion moves undertaken with their money by a business showing mediocre results and continuing with its old management.

Stock Dividends and Stock Splits

There is no confusion in the academic world, but in the world of practical finance, these terms may be used incorrectly, hence causing confusion.

The stock split, when two or more shares replace one, is merely a restatement of the common stock structure. The purpose is to reduce the market price of the individual share to encourage wider purchase.

The "proper" stock dividend is paid to shareholders as representative of reinvested earnings in the recent past (say two years or less). This should not be confused with a cash dividend. The valued amount of the stock dividend should be transferred into the accounts from earned surplus to capital. This has the same effect as paying cash from earnings, only it's not received by the shareholder as cash; instead, it's received as more shares. Graham then highlights that a stock dividend has important tax advantages over a cash dividend.

Graham is of the strong opinion that companies need to have a written policy in place that specifies whether the company will pay a certain portion of their earnings as a cash dividend or stock dividend.

There is an argument—mostly academic but probably valid—that after a stock split, the investor has more numbers but not more value. But since psychology is a big part of practical finance, it is recognized that more numbers wins friends. And the shareholder does have the option to sell the newly awarded shares in lieu of a dividend.

CHAPTER 20
"MARGIN OF SAFETY" AS
THE CENTRAL CONCEPT OF INVESTING

CHAPTER SUMMARY

This chapter starts out by outlining the importance of the margin of safety concept for investors. It is explained by comparing the earnings yield of bonds and stocks. Graham discusses the relationship between margin of safety and diversification and how the ownership of more securities is similar to underwriting insurance. It is also argued that unconventional investments could be bought at two-thirds or less of the indicated value. Mediocre quality securities, however, can only be a sound investment for the enterprising investor.

Finally, Graham outlines five basic principles about intelligent investing, with the common thread that investing is considered sound business. A closing remark addresses how the typical investor achieves *satisfactory* results more easily than most people realize—while *superior* results are harder to achieve.

CHAPTER OUTLINE

If the secret of sound investing is to be condensed into three words, they would be:

MARGIN OF SAFETY

All experienced investors recognize the essential character of this requirement; for instance, a railroad stock should have earned its total fixed charges better than five times for its bonds to qualify as investment-grade issues. The *past* ability to earn in excess of interest requirements constitutes the margin of safety to protect against loss in a *future* decline.

For the bond investor, if the margin of safety is a large one, it is enough to assume future earnings will not fall far below those of the past in order for the investor to feel sufficiently protected against the potential changes with the passage of time.

The margin of safety of bonds may be calculated by comparing the total value of the business with its debt: if the total value is $30 million and the debt is $10 million, there is theoretical room for a shrinkage of two-thirds.

For common stock, the margin of safety is more difficult to calculate. It may happen that the common stock is found to have a margin of safety equal to that of the bond described. This is more likely to be found when the market is depressed. Usually, however, the margin of safety resides in an expected earning power considerably above that of bonds, which may, over a ten-year period, aggregate 50% of the price paid and is sufficient to provide a very real margin of safety. This is more likely if the investor has been practicing averaging buying on an annual basis, and not waiting for the top of the market before he invested his money.

When Graham gave his lecture in 1972, he defined the margin of safety as, "The difference between the percentage rate of the earnings on the stock at the price you pay for it and the rate of interest on bonds, and that margin of safety is the difference which would absorb unsatisfactory developments."

"At the time the 1965 edition was written, the typical stock was selling at eleven times earnings, giving about 9% return as against 4% on bonds. In that case, you had a margin of safety of over 100%. In the 1970s, there is no difference between the earnings rate on stocks and the interest rate on bonds, and I say there is no margin of safety."

The risk of paying too much for quality stocks, although real, is not the chief hazard; that comes from the purchase of low-quality stocks at times of favorable business conditions. The purchaser assumes prosperity is synonymous with safety. It is at such times that stocks of obscure companies are floated at prices far above tangible investment. Such stocks do not offer a margin of safety; this requires examination of a stock's performance over a number of years.

- Note: This was Graham's way of suggesting stocks need a form of past performance and stability in order to predict future earnings trends more accurately.

The growth stock investor relies on an expected earnings power that will be greater than the average shown in the past and is (mentally) substituting these anticipated earnings for margin of safety. Graham accepts this may be valid and states: "Security analysis is coming more and more to prefer a competently executed evaluation of the future; thus the growth stock approach may supply as dependable a margin of safety as is found in the ordinary investment, provided the calculation of the future is conservatively made, and provided it shows a satisfactory margin in relation to the price paid."

In a growth stock program, the danger lies in that the market has a tendency to set prices that will not be protected by a *conservative* projection of future earnings—all prudent estimates must err on the side of understanding.

Margin of safety is therefore dependent on the price paid; if the entire group is overpriced, then a portfolio of diversified buying will not solve the problem, but wise individual selections may serve the purpose.

The buyer of bargain issues has no particular enthusiasm for the issue itself; he buys only because it appears to be a bargain. He must place particular emphasis on the ability of the issue to withstand adverse conditions, being aware of the difference between market price and appraised value.

Theory of Diversification

Diversification is an established tenet of conservative investing.

Holding a single stock with a margin of safety may or may not prove satisfactory, but holding several stocks, each with a margin of safety, is more likely to do so by spreading the risk—an insurance policy.

A Criterion of Investment versus Speculation

There is no single definition of "investment."

Many will deny there is any difference between investment and speculation, so Graham suggests the concept of "margin of safety" be used to distinguish one from the other. Margin of safety rests on definable mathematical criteria.

Extension of the Concept of Investment

"Conventional" investments suitable for the conservative investor are: US Government issues, high-grade, dividend-paying common stock, State and Municipal bonds with tax-exempt features, first-quality corporate bonds if yields are greater than the US Savings Bond.

"Unconventional" investments should be considered only by the enterprising investor. The broadest category is undervalued common stocks of secondary companies, to be bought only when they are at less than two-thirds of indicated value. Another choice is medium-grade corporate bonds when selling at depressed prices with considerable discount from their apparent value. In Graham's view, a sufficiently low price raises a mediocre quality security to a sound investment opportunity, provided the buyer understands what he is doing, and is diversified. In this sense, it might be thought that there is no such thing as "good" or "bad" stock, only "cheap" and "expensive."

"Fair-weather investments" are found where speculation failed, the market collapsed. The stock or bond still represents value with a large margin of safety, raising it from the class of speculation to an investment opportunity. *(The analyst who calls a stock a "strong buy" at its peak, and a "sell" as it descends voices the opposite of Graham's long-established philosophy of "buy low and sell high.")*

"Special situations" predicated on a thorough analysis are part of this unconventional investment philosophy, but only for the enterprising investor.

To Sum Up

Investment is most intelligent when it is most *businesslike.*

Every corporate security should be viewed as taking part ownership in that business.

An intention to create profit from purchase and sales of securities is in itself a business, and should be conducted as one would conduct any other business.

The first principle is: *Know what you are doing—know your business.*

The second principle is: *Don't let other people run your business unless a) you supervise with enough care and comprehension, and b) you have unusually strong confidence in his integrity and ability.*

The third principle is: *Do not enter into manufacturing or trading, or operations like these, unless a reliable calculation shows they have a strong chance of yielding a respectable profit.*

The fourth principle is: *Keep away from ventures where you have little to gain and much to lose. Operations for profit should be based on arithmetic, not optimism.*

The fifth principle is: *Have confidence and courage in your knowledge and experience; if you have formed a conclusion from the facts, and you know your judgment is sound, then act on it. In investing, "courage becomes the supreme virtue" only after gaining adequate knowledge and tested judgment.*

In the case of the average investor, he may not need to bring all these qualities to bear on his program, provided always that:

a) He limits his ambition to his capacity.

b) He confines his activities within the safe and narrow path of standard, defensive, investment.

In Investment:

"To achieve *satisfactory* results is easier than most people realize— but to achieve *superior* results is harder than it looks."

POSTSCRIPT

Graham describes the operation of the fund he ran and reports it had an annualized profit of 20%.

Graham describes one particular investment, Government Employee Insurance Co., otherwise known as GEICO, and how, convinced of its likelihood of success, they invested 20% of the fund in that one company. Although that was not quite, "betting the farm," it does seem to be a very large investment, though Graham was confident that, at the very worst, the money invested could be recovered. As it turned out, their judgment was so correct that, "The aggregate of profits accruing from this single investment decision far exceeded the sum of all the others realized through twenty years of wide-ranging operations..."

In attempting to seek morals from this story, he points out:

a) On Wall Street there are several ways to make and keep money

b) One lucky break (or supremely shrewd decision—take your pick) may count for more than a lifetime of efforts. But one has to be ready, in position, and skilled in asset valuation to recognize and "go for" the break.

APPENDIX
The Superinvestors of
Graham-and-Doddsville

A lecture given by Warren E. Buffett at Columbia University in 1984 in which he amusingly reduces a thesis to the absurd to make his point.

A group of 225 million persons each flip a coin at sunrise for a dollar bet. Half will come up as winners—they keep the winnings and are chosen to stay in the game, with each day the losers' stakes being added to the pot. The next day, the 112.5 million repeat the flip, and half come up as winners. After ten days, there are 220,000 recurring winners, each of whom has won more than $1,000. It is to be expected that they will start boasting of their coin-flipping skills. After ten further days of flipping coins at sunrise, the 215 members of the winning group that has survived twenty flips will have won over a million dollars. It is to be expected that books entitled, *How I Turned a Dollar Into a Million in Twenty Days, Working Thirty Seconds a Morning* will appear for sale, and members of the surviving group will go on the lecture circuit describing the techniques of "efficient coin-flipping" and confronting the skeptics with their argument, "If it can't be done, why are there 215 of us?" But some business school professors might be rude enough to point out that an equal number of monkeys would have had the same results—that is to say, 215 egotistical monkeys!

Buffett then asks an important question: What if 215 winners were left after twenty days, and forty of them all came from Omaha?

Buffett goes on to state that those who were trained by Graham, as he was, have succeeded in finance not by random chance calling of the flip, but because of their careful analysis of the coin-calling decisions. Buffett concludes this funny story by stating that a firm understanding of the relationship between price and value was the variable that allowed investors to make this determination.

Near the end of Buffett's lecture, he also makes a very important comment about Benjamin Graham's guidance for margin of safety. He says, "When you build a bridge, you insist it will carry 30,000 pounds, but you only drive 10,000 pound trucks across it." Likewise, investors shouldn't settle paying $80 million for a business that's only worth $83 million.

The two primary points that Buffett discusses during the lecture are the importance of value versus price, and margin of safety.

THEMES FOUND THROUGHOUT THE BOOK

- This is not a *"How to Make a Million Dollars"* book.
- The book has been written with investors in mind, as opposed to speculators, and the first task is to distinguish between the two.
- There are no easy paths to riches on Wall Street (or anywhere else).
- The underlying principles of sound investment should not alter from decade to decade, but the application of these principles must be adapted to significant changes in the financial mechanisms and climate.
- The book distinguishes between two types of investor: The defensive or passive investor, who primarily emphasizes the avoidance of losses, and the enterprising investor, who is willing to devote the necessary time and care to the selection of securities that are more attractive than the average.
- The art of successful investment is based on first selecting the industry that is most likely to grow, then selecting the most promising company within that industry.
- Obvious prospects for physical growth in a business do not translate into obvious profits for investors. The experts do not have dependable ways of selecting and concentrating on the most promising companies in the most promising industries.
- The investor's chief problem, and his worst enemy, is likely to be himself, as he is exposed to the excitements and temptations of the stock market. More money is made and kept by ordinary people who are temperamentally suited to investment than it is by many who lack that quality despite being otherwise well informed in all the details and machinery of finance and the market.
- The intent is to teach the reader to measure and quantify. At some prices, 99% of issues are cheap enough to buy—buy stocks as if they were groceries, not perfume.
- A creditable but unspectacular result can be achieved by the lay investor with minimal effort and capability. To improve

on this easily obtainable standard requires much application and wisdom; bringing only a little knowledge and cleverness, however, is likely to worsen the situation.

- If anyone can "*match* the average," ought it not to be easy to "*beat* the average"? The proportion of smart people who fail in their attempt to do this is very large, as demonstrated by the majority of investment funds, all of which are run by "experts," yet have failed to meet the average returns of the general market.

- Emphasis throughout the book is given to the virtues of having a simple portfolio: high-grade bonds and diversified leading common stocks.

- Investment must be based on the "margin of safety" principle.

- Enthusiasm on Wall Street almost invariably leads to disaster!

- The habit of relating what is paid to what is being offered is an invaluable trait in investment.

- Investment is most intelligent when it is most *businesslike*.

- Every corporate security should be viewed as taking part ownership in that business.

- An intention to create profit from purchase and sales of securities is in itself a business, and should be conducted as one would conduct any other business.

- The first principle is: *Know what you are doing—know your business.*

- Do not let any other person run your business.

- Do not enter into any operation unless a reliable calculation shows it has a fair chance of yielding a reasonable profit.

- Keep away from ventures where you have little to gain and much to lose.

- Operations for profit should be based on arithmetic, not optimism.

- Have the courage of your knowledge and experience.

- In investing, "courage becomes the supreme virtue" only after gaining adequate knowledge and tested judgment.

- The average investor should limit his ambition to his capacity and confine his activities within the safe and narrow path of defensive investment.

ABOUT THE BOOK

The Intelligent Investor, by Benjamin Graham, was first published in 1949, and is a widely acclaimed book on *value investing*, the approach to investment that Graham began to teach at Columbia Business School in 1928. It was subsequently refined in conjunction with David Dodd, and described by Warren Buffett as, "By far the best book on investing ever written"—a view shared by Irving Kahn, Walter Schloss, and other Graham disciples.

The content of the book already existed in the earlier book, *Security Analysis*. In principle, value investing opposes the assumption that the stock market is "efficient." Graham promoted the idea of value investing: to buy stocks whose price is lower than their true value and then to hold those stocks until their price returns to the true value, thus earning a return on the investment.

The work was published in 1949; Graham revised it several times in 1959, 1965, then published in 1973 as the *Fourth Revised Edition*, and included a preface and appendices by Warren Buffett.

Graham died in 1976. Commentaries and new footnotes were added to the fourth edition by Jason Zweig, and this new revision was published in 2003.

ABOUT THE AUTHOR

Benjamin Graham was named Benjamin Grossbaum when he was born in London, England, to Jewish parents, May 8, 1894. When he was one year old, the family moved to New York City where his father dealt in china dishes and figurines. They prospered, lived on Upper Fifth Avenue, and had maidservants and a French governess for young Benjamin. But his father died in 1903, the business failed and the home was made into a boarding house run by his mother, Dorothy, who borrowed money to trade on margin and was wiped out financially—all of which can only have left a very deep impression of the dangers of the market on her son. Although they suffered from poverty when his father died, Benjamin won a scholarship to Columbia University where at the age of twenty he graduated second in his class and was class salutatorian. Although offered a post as an instructor in mathematics and other subjects, he entered the finance field in 1914.

During World War I, it was considered expedient to change the name from the Germanic "Grossbaum" to the Scottish "Graham."

On Wall Street, he was initially a clerk in a bond-trading firm, then became an analyst, a partner, and eventually started the Graham-Newman Partnership, an open-end mutual fund that was later closed to new investors.

Although he had his triumphs in personal investing, he suffered, as did many others, in the "Great Crash" of 1929-32, and sustained 70% losses. His corporation, the Graham-Newman Partnership, had one of the best long-term records in history, and reported annual earnings of 14.7% compared with 12.2% for the market.

Graham is considered the first proponent of value investing, an investment approach he began teaching at Columbia Business School in 1928 and subsequently refined with David Dodd through various editions of their famous book, *Security Analysis*. The book was published in 1934 and has been considered a bible for serious investors since it was written.

Security Analysis and *The Intelligent Investor,* the latter of which was published in 1949, are his two most widely acclaimed books. In *Security Analysis*, he proposed a clear definition of investment that was distinguished from what he deemed speculation.

Graham exhorted the stock market participant to first draw a fundamental distinction between investment and speculation. He was critical of the corporations of his day for hiding the underlying meaning of financial reports and information. He was an advocate of businesses making dividend payments to shareholders rather than keeping all of their profits as retained earnings.

Graham's favorite allegory is that of Mr. Market, a fellow who turns up every day at the stock holder's door offering to buy or sell his shares at a different price. Usually, the price quoted by Mr. Market seems plausible, but occasionally it is ridiculous. The investor is free to either agree with his quoted price and trade with him, or to ignore him completely. Mr. Market doesn't mind this, and will be back the following day to quote another price. The point is that the investor should not regard the whims of Mr. Market as determining the value of the shares that the investor owns. He should profit from market folly rather than participate in it. The investor is best off concentrating on the real-life performance of his companies, and receiving dividends, rather than being too concerned with Mr. Market's often irrational behavior.

Buffett, who credits Graham as grounding him with a sound intellectual investment framework, described him as the second most influential person in his life after his own father, and wrote, "A remarkable aspect of Ben's dominance of his professional field was that he achieved it without that narrowness of mental activity that concentrates all effort on a single end. It was, rather, the incidental by-product of an intellect whose breadth almost exceeded definition. Certainly I have never met anyone with a mind of similar scope. Virtually total recall, unending fascination with new knowledge, and an ability to recast it in a form applicable to seemingly unrelated problems made exposure to his thinking in any field a delight."

According to Warren Buffett, Graham said that he wished every day to do something foolish, something creative, and something generous. Buffett said that Graham excelled most at the last.

He died September 21, 1976, in Aix-en-Provence, France.

Graham is the author of:

Security Analysis, editions 1934, 1940, 1951, 1962, 1988, 2008

The Intelligent Investor, editions 1949, reprinted in 2005; 1959, 1965, 1973

Storage and Stability: A Modern Ever-Normal Granary, New York: McGraw-Hill, 1937

The Interpretation of Financial Statements

World Commodities and World Currency, 1944

Benjamin Graham, the Memoirs of the Dean of Wall Street

THE SUMMARY AUTHORS

Preston Pysh is a leadership and financial investing author. He has published multiple international best selling books and is the founder of the Pylon Holding Company. He runs the free educational website, BuffettsBooks.com, which teaches students how to invest in stocks and bonds like the billionaire Warren Buffett.

Author of
The Diary of a West Point Cadet
Warren Buffett's Three Favorite Books
Warren Buffett Accounting Book
A Summary of the Intelligent Investor

Stig Brodersen holds a master's degree in Finance and has studied Business Analysis at Harvard University. Stig works as a college professor teaching a variety of courses including financial accounting, investment and economics. Stig also owns the investment company Stig Brodersen Holding and is a co-founder of the free educational website, BuffettsBooks.com.

Author of
Warren Buffett Accounting Book
A Summary of the Intelligent Investor

Made in the USA
San Bernardino, CA
06 July 2018